TRAVELLING THE WORLD AS CITIZENS OF HEAVEN

STEPHEN LIGGINS

matthiasmedia
SYDNEY • YOUNGSTOWN

Travelling the World as Citizens of Heaven

Matthias Media
(St Matthias Press Ltd ACN 067 558 365)
Email: info@matthiasmedia.com.au
Internet: www.matthiasmedia.com.au
Please visit our website for current postal and telephone contact information.

Matthias Media (USA)
Email: sales@matthiasmedia.com
Internet: www.matthiasmedia.com
Please visit our website for current postal and telephone contact information.

In various anecdotes within these pages, names and incidental details have often been changed to protect the privacy of certain individuals.

ISBN 978 1 925424 11 9

Cover design and typesetting by Lankshear Design.

To Mum, Dad, Eva and Veloo

CONTENTS

WHO THIS BOOK IS FOR AND WHY I WROTE IT

This book is for Christians who are thinking about travelling or living abroad, and for those who are already doing it. It may be for a few weeks' holiday, a backpacking adventure, a visit to family or friends, a gap year, a working holiday, a sabbatical, a study trip, a ministry trip, a work transfer, or any combination of the above. This book is also for Christian family, friends and church workers who are supporting or advising someone who's considering going overseas or is already abroad.

I am an evangelical minister who works for a church in the Blue Mountains just outside of Sydney in Australia. I'm also a guest lecturer at the Sydney Missionary and Bible College, I write short pieces on evangelism for a Christian website, and I've recently written an academic book on the book of Acts. So why would I write a book about Christians travelling and living overseas, instead of tackling a more 'significant' topic?

Well, while it is far from being the most important thing in my life, I do love travelling and spending time in foreign lands. I moved from Sydney to London for five months when I was 20 years old in an effort to kickstart a career in cricket. While there I got involved with a large evangelical church, and God used that trip to bring about great spiritual growth in my life. In the years since that first trip I've left Australia a number of times—for short-term backpacking and other holidays, for work, and for ministry. For me, travelling and living overseas has been a great positive for my Christian life.

But for all the potential benefits and joys of going abroad, I am very aware of its perils for the Christian. In thinking about whether to go and in planning our travels, there is a real danger that we will think and act in accordance with the world's agenda instead of God's. There are important questions to address—for example, is the trip a wise use of money and time? How will this time away impact my relationships, church and ministry? Furthermore, being away from home, church and normal routine for an extended period can play havoc with one's Christian life. You may know people whose faith has been shipwrecked on foreign shores.

There is a range of views in the Christian community about the wisdom, merits and dangers of going to foreign lands for any length of time other than for full-time missionary service. Travel certainly does present many opportunities and pitfalls for the believer abroad. I believe that where damage occurs, much of it results from the fact that Christians have gone away unwisely or spiritually unprepared. We can spend so much time and energy planning itineraries and organizing details that we don't give any thought to our devotional life or to Christian fellowship. Conversely, wise, godly consideration and preparation can lead to a highly positive and productive experience.

Given the fact that more and more people these days are travelling and living overseas, and since to my knowledge no other book has been written on the topic of Christians and travel, it seemed good to put my fingers to the keyboard. This book aims to help Christians think wisely about whether to travel, how to travel, and particularly how to think and act when away from home. It seeks to do this in a biblically sound, ethically wise, and interesting way, drawing on my own thoughts and experiences as well as those of other travellers, Christian workers and parents. My hope is that if a believer does venture abroad, the experience will be a spiritual plus rather than a spiritual minus—a real help to their faith, not a hindrance.

INTRODUCTION

Where can I go from your Spirit?
Where can I flee from your presence?
If I go up to the heavens, you are there;
if I make my bed in the depths, you are there.
If I rise on the wings of the dawn,
if I settle on the far side of the sea,
even there your hand will guide me,
your right hand will hold me fast. (Ps 139:7-10)

Take off!

I never expected to travel—well, not overseas anyway. Growing up, family holidays were local affairs: five-in-a-station-wagon Aussie odysseys involving tents, air mattresses and a portable stove. Overseas destinations seemed unattainably exotic. At school I did unnecessarily detailed projects on foreign lands such as 'Europe' and 'Scandinavia', but these were distant and magical worlds I was never likely to inhabit. International travel seemed about as likely for me as the kind of travel that featured in another hopelessly extravagant assignment I submitted to my fifth-grade teacher, entitled 'Astronauts'.

But life has a way of throwing up its surprises, and the unexpected can happen. For here I was one early evening in April, aged 20, sitting in a plane on the tarmac at Sydney preparing to take off for London. London! I was ecstatic.

My entry to the world of travelling and living overseas was accidental. I had hopes of becoming a professional cricketer, and, as a Christian, I thought the world could do with a few more prominent believers in that sport. So I'd taken time off from university to play cricket with a club side in London for five months, hoping to improve my game.

The club would provide my accommodation but I needed money for my airfare and living expenses, so I'd spent my weekdays for the previous few months working as a helper in a children's holiday play centre, and as a linen distributive engineer and bed-composition technician (let the reader understand) in a local retirement complex. In the evenings I planned what I needed to take and how I might go about living away from home. Partway through this process it dawned on me that I would also have the opportunity to look around parts of the UK and maybe even Europe.

Minutes earlier I had farewelled family and friends at the airport. It was a poignant moment—until then my longest stretch away from home had been two weeks in Melbourne (where I'd been homesick), and here I was moving hemispheres for five months! But a lot of people were supporting me and praying for me, including my parents and the church fellowship group I attended. The senior minister at my church had given me the details of two good churches in London, and my friends were excited about what I was doing. A few came out to the airport to see me off, and one even slipped me an encouraging note and a couple of evangelistic tracts.

A thousand thoughts were swirling in my head as, after what seemed like interminable taxiing, the plane finally started down the runway, gathering speed until it finally broke contact with the earth's surface and we were airborne.

I still love planes—the novelty is yet to wear off. Almost every flight is taking me somewhere exciting or interesting, or to do something worthwhile. The weeks of frenzied preparations finally give way to a floating world in which all you can do is sit, talk, read, pray, think, watch movies, listen to music or sleep, as pleasant flight attendants bring you one meal after another. It is an oasis of rest.

That April evening, I found myself sitting with Amelia and Scott. Amelia was a member of the New Zealand women's underwater hockey team. (Yes, I know. I thought I knew sport, but this was a new one for me, too.) Scott was a lawyer from Melbourne. We chatted easily and intermittently throughout the flight. I thought of giving them the two tracts but, perhaps lacking a little courage, didn't.

Cruising through the night, the flight set down temporarily in Perth, where I met a Christian called Andrew. A friend had tipped me off that Andrew would be on the plane, describing him as "5 foot 10 with blond hair". My enthusiasm levels were running high enough that this was sufficient information for me to track him down on a plane full of hundreds of passengers. He was the first of many believers I would meet on my travels.

Hours later, the sun rose over Sri Lanka and we started to descend into Madras (now Chennai) for refuelling. As our altitude dropped, a very different world from the one in which I'd spent my life came into view. I saw alien factories, strange housing estates… and slums. We landed and taxied to a halt. Somewhat sleep-deprived but needing to stretch my legs, I stumbled off the plane and into the humid air on the tarmac. When I reached the air-conditioned comfort of the airport terminal, I noticed soldiers carrying machine guns.

After walking aimlessly for a while I wandered, half comatose, into the men's bathroom. Before I realized what had hit me, I was surrounded by a mob of men thrusting soap and towels into my face. I was utterly disoriented. Just managing to kick a bit of grey matter into gear, I realized that they were trying to earn money, and that my wallet was back on the plane so I had nothing to give them. Panicking, I pushed my way back out into the terminal with a feeling of guilt.

I returned with relief to the familiar Western interior of the plane and thought back over what had happened. Outside, the slums—a sea of poverty—ran right up to the airport. A boy stood on a rubbish heap staring at our plane. Sadly, it seemed to me that his was a world from which there was very little chance of escape—if you were born in a slum, there you would live and there you would die.

We were soon back in the air, chasing the sun around the world. We flew over the deserts and oases of the Middle East, the hills, towns and fields of Turkey, and then the patchwork farmland, alps and cities of Europe. During the flight I had been reading *God's Smuggler*—the biography of Brother Andrew, who helped smuggle Bibles into communist Europe in the 1950s and 1960s. Now here I was looking down on those very countries where he'd worked. I wondered how the gospel was going down there now.

With my forehead pressed against the cold pane of glass,

I looked down and marvelled that in each of the tiny houses below were people who were important to God. It seemed incredible that he was interested in each of their lives, and that he heard all of their prayers.

The plane flew on and the hours ticked by. My anticipation increased as we approached England—as did the cloud. Eventually, we dropped through the mist and I got my first glimpse of London. Even from the air it looked un-Australian and very English—with duller light, trees of a deeper green, narrower streets, and rows of terraces. This was the land I'd read about and seen in movies and on television. It was the land of Dickens, the royals, the Beatles, and cricket. And I was here!

Avoiding turbulence

This was the start of five months that God used to change my life for the better. Although my cricket improved only marginally, my relationship with God grew enormously. I prayed and meditated on Scripture. I joined a large evangelical church and met many Christians both there and elsewhere. I had good opportunities to talk about my faith with nonbelievers. I also learned a lot about God, the world he created, and the fallen nature of this world. Those five months proved to be one of the most stimulating and influential periods of my life. Opportunities I've had since then to travel and work overseas have had a positive impact on my Christian life as well. And I've met many others for whom this has also been the case.

But it is not like that for everyone. I know of one Australian university student, for example, who decided to study in

Japan for six months. He was a new Christian, and before he left his Christian friends tried to connect him with a missionary working in Japan. But while he was away, his newfound Christian faith increasingly took a back seat. He didn't go to a church, his prayer and Bible reading became increasingly erratic, and his focus moved further and further away from God. He did many things he now wishes he hadn't, and hurt people in the process. Sadly, stories like this are quite common. Fortunately, this particular young man is back on track with God, but there are many others who have strayed away and stayed away.

So I am very aware of the dangers of travel for the Christian. Our decision to go overseas may be poorly made—there are good reasons to travel abroad but there are often good reasons to stay put. In our planning, we might listen to the world more than to God. We may give little thought to how we will grow in our faith while we're away from home. And while living in foreign lands, our lifestyle may bear little resemblance to that of a follower of Jesus. Being away from home, church and our usual accountability structures can tempt us to behave completely differently from the way in which we normally would.

A friend who's involved with a ministry to university students once told me that about half of the Christian students he knows who have travelled or lived overseas for a period of time have gone backwards in their faith during their time away. Of the other half, some have grown; but many have gone neither backwards nor forwards. It is a shame that they have not all grown a lot!

Part of the problem seems to be that few people talk about the very real tests and temptations that travel presents. It's easy to come to the subject of travel with an unquestionably worldly perspective, because most people in Western society speak only in glowing terms about it. As a result, Christians often travel without godly consideration and preparation. We need to be wise, however, and examine the challenging questions surrounding travel through a biblical lens.

The aims of this book, then, are to help Christians decide whether or not they should travel or live abroad (see especially chapter 7), and to help those who do decide to travel—for whatever reason and for however long—to prepare themselves spiritually so they can make the most of the opportunities and be aware of the potential struggles that lie ahead.

The itinerary

As we embark on our journey through this book, where are we going? What is our itinerary? Well, the account of my first trip to London raised many of the ideas we're going to think about. In chapter 1 we will consider what it means to travel with God. He is our Lord overseas just as much as he is when we are at home… thank goodness! No matter where we are in our travels, no matter what situation we find ourselves in, God is there.

In chapter 2 we will reflect on travelling God's world. As travel blogs, books and documentaries attest, our planet is an amazing place. Why? Because God made it and everything in it. Creation reflects God's glory. Viewing what we see and encounter in the light of this truth can transform our time away.

Then in the following two chapters we'll think about the

connections we might make with the people we meet on our travels. When we meet Christians (chapter 3), we can encourage them in their faith and, in turn, be encouraged by them. When we meet non-Christians (chapter 4), we can point them towards Christ. Every encounter is an opportunity that we can take—or lose. These chapters also discuss the positive and negative impact that other people can have on us.

The world *is* an amazing place—a masterpiece. But it's a ruined masterpiece, so in chapter 5 we address the reality of travelling in a fallen world. When we travel we'll see things that disappoint us, that shock us, and that may even devastate us. We need to prepare ourselves, as much as we can, to understand and respond to the tragedies we encounter. The best way to do this is by seeking to understand what the Bible teaches about living in a fallen world.

In chapter 6 we'll think about *how* to travel. There are all sorts of decisions to be made relating to the manner of travelling and living overseas. For example, should we travel or live alone or with another person? Should we go on a group tour or make our own plans? Does the Bible have anything to say about how we establish a travel budget? Should we aim to cover as much territory as possible or spend more time in a few different places? What steps should we take regarding safety?

In chapter 7 I raise the sometimes vexing question of whether or not we *should* travel. Travel is not a right or a necessity. We do not need to travel or live in another country, even if the expectation of our family or social set is that we will. As Christians, we want to take our cues from the Scriptures and not from the world about us. It's important to consider our reasons for travel, the stewardship issues involved, and the impact it will have on our relationships. It may seem odd to end the book with this preliminary question of whether or not to travel, but one of the reasons for doing so is that the discussions in chapters 1-6 about the pros and cons of travel may help us to grapple with this question. There are good reasons to go abroad. There are good reasons to stay home. Despite its placement, however, for some this may be the first chapter they will want to read.

And finally in the conclusion we will tie together some of the thoughts from earlier chapters and cast a vision for putting Christ first, both in our home country and (should we leave its borders) overseas.

Your fellow traveller

When you meet another traveller and you've told each other where you've been and where you're going, you often share a bit about your lives. So, since we'll be travelling together through this book, let me tell you a bit about myself. Thanks to God, I am a Christian. When I was about ten years old I asked Jesus to forgive me, and said that I wanted to follow him. Over time my faith has deepened and developed, and my life has had its up and downs, but I have never regretted becoming a Christian.

These days I am married with two children. I serve God as a minister in a church just outside of Sydney. I've also worked as a lawyer and in the Christian media, and engaged in graduate and postgraduate study. As a young man I had aspirations of becoming a professional cricketer, and I came close but did not quite pull it off. And throughout all of this, and for various reasons, I've travelled.

I'm often amazed at how going and living overseas has featured in my life even though I never really planned it that way. But having had the opportunity, I do love travelling. I love the preparation—researching the trip, purchasing essential items, and anticipating what lies ahead. I love the airports—melting pots of culture with departure boards full of promise and possibility. I love the travel itself, with the chance it gives me to sit and talk or simply fall asleep. I love arriving in a new place—working out the lie of the land, discovering cultural nuances, dealing with the unexpected, and exploring natural wonders as well as products of human ingenuity. I love meeting people—fellow travellers and locals, people who share my beliefs and those who don't. Afterwards I love reflecting back on a trip—the photos, the new friends, and the opportunity to pray for and respond to needs that have come across my path. Most of all, I love the fact that God is there with me through all of this—that he teaches me things, and that in his mercy he uses me.

As I have said, my first trip involved living in London for five months to further a career in professional cricket. While there I took the opportunity to poke around the UK, and also made a few short forays to the Continent and Scandinavia.

Three years later, when a career in cricket had not transpired and I'd finished university but hadn't yet started work, I had the opportunity to embark upon the sort of extended overseas trip that future full-time employment would not allow. But I found myself thinking and praying long and hard about it. As a Christian, was this a wise use of my money? Was it a wise use of my time? What about relationships at home? What about the coming cricket season? In the end, although I could have gone for much longer, I decided to head off for nine weeks with my backpack and an around-the-world ticket. I travelled to southern Africa and Europe and visited friends in the UK before dropping in on my eldest brother, who was then living in Texas, on my way home.

Since entering full-time employment, by using my annual leave strategically, travelling on a budget, adjusting my spending in other areas (e.g. buying cheaper cars) and tacking short holidays onto overseas work or ministry trips, I have now visited around 40 countries. I've spent time in Australia, Europe, Africa, Asia, the Middle East, the Pacific and North America. As I've grown older I've tended to travel with friends (and since 2005 with my wife), and have even gone on the occasional short organized tour.

I've met hundreds of people, witnessed many awe-inspiring sights, and seen some of the best and worst of life on this planet. In my travels I've experienced happiness and sadness, and at times I've been lonely. But in every place and situation I take encouragement from the truth summarized in what I now consider to be my travel verses:

> Where can I go from your Spirit?
>   Where can I flee from your presence?
> If I go up to the heavens, you are there;
>   if I make my bed in the depths, you are there.
> If I rise on the wings of the dawn,
>   if I settle on the far side of the sea,
> even there your hand will guide me,
>   your right hand will hold me fast. (Ps 139:7-10)

The ultimate trip

You don't have to travel very far before you start to hear the following sorts of conversations. Let's say you've arrived in South-East Asia—Thailand, perhaps. You've been on the beach for hours and then, feeling well rested, you head to a cafe to check your emails. You strike up a conversation with a guy at a neighbouring table and tell him about your day. "Yes," he replies, "Thailand is good, but it's too full of package tourists these days. If you want something less commercial, try Vietnam."

You take his advice and go to Vietnam. Once there, you decide it would be good to learn something about the local culture, so you catch a taxi and spend the day exploring some ancient temples. While cooking your two-minute noodles in the communal kitchen at the hostel that evening you fall into conversation with another traveller, who is cutting up bamboo shoots. You ask her about her day and then tell her a bit about what you've seen. "Well, yes," she admits, "there's lots to see in Vietnam, but..." and here she shrugs her shoulders, "don't you think the ice-cream stalls and souvenir shops detract from the experience? For something a bit more genuine, you should check out Laos".

A week later, you find yourself trekking in the hills in the north of Laos, staying in village huts and buying your food in markets from the local Hmong people. One day you spot another backpacker resting under a tree. Seeing a kindred spirit you decide to stop and swap travel stories. You offer him some of your snake wine and start to tell him about where you've been. He looks around with a jaded expression. "Ah, yah, Laos is okay," he concedes, "but it has become too touristic. For real authenticity, one must see Myanmar."

Many travellers are looking for that ultimate experience—the most out-of-the-way location, the most genuine religious encounter, the most adrenalin-pumping activity, the most self-actualizing relationship. Others simply head off in pursuit of pleasure, or to escape, or because they can't think of anything else to do.

Contrary to what some people think, however, travel is not the ultimate trip in life. Knowing God is. Idolizing travel will ultimately lead to disappointment and disaster. As Augustine wrote of God almost 2000 years ago: "You have made us for yourself, and our heart is restless until it rests in you".[1]

Our ultimate need is to have our sins forgiven and to be reconciled to God. Jesus, at unimaginable personal cost, died on the cross and rose from the dead to offer us forgiveness of sins, a restored relationship with God, eternal life, and numerous other benefits (and responsibilities). We receive this gift and embark on the ultimate trip by asking Jesus to forgive us and by promising to follow him.[2]

As followers of Jesus, we need to put God and his concerns first in our lives. Jesus teaches us to "seek first his kingdom and his righteousness, and all these things will be given to you as well" (Matt 6:33). This is the same priority we find in the first of the Ten Commandments: "You shall have no other gods before me" (Exod 20:3).

As Christians we know these truths, but as we live in this world and perhaps move within the travel community,

1 Augustine, *Confessions*, book I, chapter 1, trans. H Chadwick, OUP, Oxford, 2009, p. 3.
2 For a fuller gospel explanation see the appendix, 'Two Ways to Live'.

it is possible for contrary attitudes to creep in. Almost imperceptibly, we can move from enjoying travel as part of our Christian life, to viewing travel and Christianity as parts of our life, until finally we find ourselves fitting Christianity in around our travels.

For followers of Jesus, *Christianity is our life*. Travel may or may not be part of that, but if it is then it needs to be firmly under the lordship of Jesus. As we read and apply God's word, God guides us in how we should order our priorities. The Holy Spirit, who lives within and is the constant companion of every believer, empowers us in this. The Spirit helps us to overcome sin (Rom 8:13) and to display good Christian character (Gal 5:22-23). Our primary aim as believers is to love God and love others. We want to become more like Jesus and to do what we can to help people become Christians and grow as Christians. These priorities, combined with our own personal circumstances, will inform not only how we travel but also our decisions about whether to travel at all.

We don't *need* to travel or live overseas. While I love travelling abroad, I would have done perfectly well without it. Travelling is not the ultimate trip. The ultimate trip is following Jesus, and we are privileged to have Jesus as our travel guide.

1

TRAVELLING WITH GOD

> *"I am the vine; you are the branches. If you remain in me and I in you, you will bear much fruit; apart from me you can do nothing."* (John 15:5)

The train sat, stationary, in the sparsely wooded grasslands of northern Botswana. Minutes had turned into hours, and it was starting to get dark. I'd boarded that morning in Zimbabwe for what was meant to be a four-hour trip across the border to Francistown, Botswana's second largest city. I'd planned to stay overnight there before catching a bus to Maun, near the edge of the Okavango Delta—the massive inland delta in the north-west of the country.

The train had been scheduled to arrive in Francistown around mid-afternoon. This would have given me time to organize some accommodation while it was still light and then take a pleasant evening's stroll before having dinner and turning in for the night. But in Africa, Western ideas of schedules and travel plans are more like aspirational goals than an indication of anything that's necessarily going to happen.

A few hours earlier, without warning, we had ground to a halt somewhere between the border and our destination. We were stranded in what looked to me like the middle of nowhere (and believe me, as an Australian I understand what it is to be in the middle of nowhere). The land was flat, the vegetation scrubby, the sun hot and the soil dry. One hour became two, then three, then four. Surprisingly, no-one in the carriage seemed in the slightest bit bothered by this turn of events. They simply sat, ate, and talked. It was as if they had never expected to get to Francistown on time, and this was all simply part of the program. (Years later, in Uganda, I heard of a Westerner who was doing postgraduate study on African administration. If you've ever been to Africa you'll appreciate what an interesting topic that would be for a Westerner, given the cross-cultural differences with respect to relationships, time and priorities.)

Sitting on the train I had plenty of time to think, and it slowly began to dawn on me that if we ever reached our destination, it would be well after dark. Even though I'm 194 centimetres tall (6'4"), and had by that time somewhat acclimatized to Africa, a hurried search for a bed under the cover of darkness in an alien city had me on the edge of my comfort zone. My tension levels began to rise. Peaceful reflection on God morphed into a growing awareness of my reliance on him. Of course, God is always present and we always need him, but in those circumstances I was especially conscious of his presence and of my need.

I prayed, and remembered my travel verses—Psalm

139:7-10. God was here in Botswana just as he was in Sydney and London and wherever else. Here on the far side of the sea, his hand would guide and hold me fast. I found myself mentally singing a Christian song I'd learned years earlier: "Jehovah Jireh, my provider, his grace is sufficient for me, for me, for me..." I knew that God would provide for all my needs and that his angels would watch over me. Thoughts of God's presence, protection and guidance were a great comfort.

Eventually after seven hours, and again without warning, the train ground to a slow start and gradually picked up speed. It was 10.30pm when we pulled into Francistown. I disembarked into the darkness, fought my way through a crowd of men hawking various things, and made my way towards the nearest hotel. I did not know it then, but God had a surprise in store for me. That night in the foyer I met an English girl, Kate, who told me she was a Christian and had recommitted her life to Christ six weeks earlier at a Billy Graham crusade in London. Although it was late, we had a long talk and encouraged each other in our shared faith. Had the train run on time, we may never have met.

Our relationship with God

One of the great encouragements and comforts we have as Christians is the fact that God is always with us—reminding us of his presence, reassuring us, orchestrating the events of our lives, and working for our good whatever the circumstances. No matter where we are, no matter what situation we find ourselves in, he is still within us and around us. But when we're travelling or living overseas it's easy to overlook or downplay his presence, so we need to keep asking ourselves how our relationship with God is going.

To say that our relationship with God is important is like saying that air is important. Our relationship with God is absolutely crucial; it is what life is all about. It is what we were created for—our hearts are restless until they find their rest in him! As Christians we have committed ourselves to following Jesus, and that means knowing him, relating to him, and becoming like him. Whether we are at home or travelling, this relationship is foundational to our existence. A close relationship with God brings glory to God. It's good for others and it's good for us.

Jesus talks about this relationship in his teaching about the vine and the branches in John 15, saying to his followers:

> 4 "Remain in me, as I also remain in you. No branch can bear fruit by itself; it must remain in the vine. Neither can you bear fruit unless you remain in me.
>
> 5 "I am the vine; you are the branches. If you remain
> in me and I in you, you will bear much fruit; apart
> from me you can do nothing. 6 If you do not remain in
> me, you are like a branch that is thrown away and
> withers; such branches are picked up, thrown into the
> fire and burned. 7 If you remain in me and my words
> remain in you, ask whatever you wish, and it will be
> done for you. 8 This is to my Father's glory, that you
> bear much fruit, showing yourselves to be my disciples.
>
> 9 "As the Father has loved me, so have I loved you.
> Now remain in my love. 10 If you keep my commands,
> you will remain in my love, just as I have kept my
> Father's commands and remain in his love. 11 I have

told you this so that my joy may be in you and that your joy may be complete. [12] My command is this: Love each other as I have loved you. [13] Greater love has no one than this: to lay down one's life for one's friends. [14] You are my friends if you do what I command. [15] I no longer call you servants, because a servant does not know his master's business. Instead, I have called you friends, for everything that I learned from my Father I have made known to you. [16] You did not choose me, but I chose you and appointed you so that you might go and bear fruit—fruit that will last—and so that whatever you ask in my name the Father will give you. [17] This is my command: Love each other." (John 15:4-17)

We experience relationships at many different levels. There are people we know—people we meet for a few days while travelling, for example. There are those we know well, such as close friends we've known for years. Then there are those very close relationships, between parents and children or husbands and wives. In John 15 Jesus says that he loves us (v. 9) and that we are his friends (vv. 14-15), but the mutual indwelling described between Jesus and his followers here goes even deeper: we are *in* Jesus (and must remain so) and he is *in* us (vv. 4-5).

All relationships require and thrive on communication. Imagine travelling or living with someone who never listened to you or spoke to you. It would be both disappointing and frustrating (not to mention weird). But when we are overseas this is sometimes how we treat God, who is our constant companion. Like all relationships, our relationship with God requires communication. We need to listen to him (v. 14) and pray to him (v. 7). On the road, just as when we're at home, we need to be in regular communication with God.

Our relationship with God also has a purpose. Jesus says that if we remain in him we will "bear much fruit" (v. 5). "Fruit" might be understood as those attitudes or actions that bring glory to God. Such attitudes would include the fruit of the Spirit (Gal 5:22-23), and such actions would include testifying to our faith. The world in which we live and travel badly needs Christians to display fruit of this sort.

A close relationship with God involves *reading, reflecting, relating, relying* and *applying*. I've almost always found myself growing in each of these five areas while I've been overseas. When we're away from our regular routines and commitments we can often set aside more time for *reading* God's word, *reflecting* on what it says, and *relating* to God in prayer. Being away from the comfort and safety of home can also encourage us to *rely* on God more and provide a myriad of opportunities for *applying* God's word. The unfortunate flip side of all this is that things can also work the other way. Away from our normal support structures and accountability partners, we can become slack in reading, reflecting and relating. We think we are too busy. We get out of our normal routines. And when our relationship with God becomes distant, bad patterns emerge in the way we rely on and apply God's word.

So let me encourage you: if you travel or move overseas, resolve to do so with God.

In this chapter, we'll consider each of these five aspects of our relationship with God and his word. Along the way we'll also discuss three things that can help us in this relationship: church and Christian fellowship, time to think, and 'Christian' locations.

Reading, reflecting and relating

Reading God's word is a fundamental part of our relationship with him. His word is where he has revealed himself, so if we want to know God and his will for our lives then that's where we must go. The Scriptures will also change us—as the writer to the Hebrews points out:

> For the word of God is alive and active. Sharper than any double-edged sword, it penetrates even to dividing soul and spirit, joints and marrow; it judges the thoughts and attitudes of the heart. (Heb 4:12)

It is essential, then, to maintain your quiet times (or personal devotions)[3] wherever you are, and being abroad can actually aid you in this—particularly if you're travelling alone or with another believer. If you're not on a package tour, you can set your own schedule and priorities, and there's no real opposition to you setting aside time to be with God. Indeed, there are often long periods when you're travelling by public transport or waiting at bus or train stations that are tailor-made for Bible reading, reflection and prayer. Similarly, if you're living overseas it's possible that you will find quiet times easier to maintain since you're likely to have fewer commitments outside of work than you do back at home.

Things may be a little more challenging if you're travelling

3 For a number of years, one of my ambitions has been to serve the Christian community by coming up with a phrase that describes a daily time of Bible reading, reflection and prayer other than 'quiet time', which sounds quaint and passive, or 'personal devotion', which strikes me as a little early-20th century. I've searched for an alternative term but to no avail (my 'meaningful interaction with God' never got much traction—with myself or with anyone else!). For lack of a better phrase, I'll use these terms so that at least you'll know what I'm talking about.

or living with a nonbeliever, but this isn't an insurmountable obstacle. If your companion knows you're a Christian, they will probably expect you to be doing things like reading your Bible and praying. After all, that's what Christians do, isn't it? Sometimes Christians can be more self-conscious than non-Christians about these sorts of things.

Setting aside time to spend with God can be more challenging if you're travelling as part of an organized tour. Tours are often packed with activities from dawn until late into the night, and peer pressure can be strong. If there's another Christian on the tour with you, you can keep each other accountable. I have two Christian friends, John and Brad, who did exactly that on a package tour of Europe for 18 to 35-year-olds a few years ago. Sometimes they had their quiet times in their rooms and at other times on the tour bus. Another Christian friend, Robbie, who travelled with a tour group in South-East Asia by himself, told me that sometimes he found it easy to have his quiet time and sometimes it was difficult, but he disciplined himself to do it.

Your regular time of reading, reflecting and praying may last anywhere from five minutes to an hour or longer, but the main thing is to do it. Obviously, you need to have a Bible with you—either in print or on your phone or tablet. No matter how lightly you're travelling, you cannot do without this item. Of course, an electronic version is very light and can be read at night without external illumination, but print versions can also be both small and light. Some people just prefer reading a hard copy—and it never runs out of charge.

Here's an idea: why not set yourself a Bible-reading challenge for your time abroad? You could read through a large section of Scripture to help you grasp the big picture of

God's purposes—say, the four Gospels (Matthew, Mark, Luke and John). Or you might decide to get to know a smaller section of Scripture really well—perhaps the Sermon on the Mount (Matthew 5-7). You could explore a particular theme in Scripture—grace, encouragement, judgement or evangelism. You may find it helpful to use Bible-reading notes or a daily devotional booklet. There are lots of good resources that are appropriate for travel. One girl told me she loaded some travel devotionals onto her phone before she left to go overseas. We plan so many other aspects of our trips—why not plan our Bible reading and reflection as well?

As we know, quiet times are a two-way street: we listen to God (reading and reflecting), but we also speak to him (relating). If you're someone who struggles with knowing what to pray for, you may find it helpful to structure your daily prayers. There are many ways of doing this—for example, there's the ACTS formula (adoration, confession, thanksgiving, supplication). You can pray for different points in each category on different days of the week (e.g. I pray for different friends on different days). This is just one suggestion for how to organize your prayers—you need to figure out what works for you. And of course we shouldn't limit prayer to any specific list or time. We can speak to God anywhere, about anything, at any time of the day or night.

Church and Christian fellowship

> And let us consider how we may spur one another on toward love and good deeds, not giving up meeting together, as some are in the habit of doing, but

> encouraging one another—and all the more as you see the Day approaching. (Heb 10:24-25)

Since the earliest times, Christians have met together to hear God's word, to pray, and to have fellowship (Acts 2:42). Meeting together is one of the chief ways by which we grow in our relationship with God.

I grew up in a large evangelical church in Sydney, where the Bible was taught well and the good news about Jesus Christ was front and centre. I became a Christian at around the age of ten, and from that time I really enjoyed the children's, youth, and young adults' ministries. When I was about 16, I began to find the evening services at church stimulating and helpful. There was some really good teaching and the music was great. So when I arrived in London a few years later, there was no way I was going to neglect meeting with other believers simply because I was in another country.

As I mentioned earlier, the senior minister at my church in Sydney had given me the details of two churches in London. I thanked him at the time, but I remember being slightly surprised. I figured I'd simply attend a good local church near my accommodation. So on my first Sunday morning in London I set off to attend a church near where I was living. I can't remember much about it but according to my diary I was "too scared" to go in to this church that "seemed to have a congregation of a few old people". I imagine it must have been the differences in architecture, size, and demographic that threw me. My church in Sydney met in a relatively modern building, and there were people of all ages in the congregation. Still, I must have realized as I wrote in my diary later on that not going in was the result of an attitude problem on my part. "This is the 'What can church do for *me*' attitude", I recorded. Thus self-chastised, I decided not to make the same mistake again.

The following Sunday morning, I tried another local church. It was a lovely old traditional building, and quite large. I decided to hit the 8am service. The small congregation consisted mostly of older people, and to my surprise the service was a short 30-minute affair. I don't remember if there was singing, and I'm not sure if there was a sermon. I met and talked with someone afterwards but left feeling somewhat bewildered. This was nothing like the church life to which I was accustomed.

Around that time, I met a vicar in a social context. Enthusiastically, I told him that I was a Christian and went to church in Australia, but he appeared somewhat underwhelmed. I was beginning to sense that things were perhaps a little different in London.

But I would not be deterred, and I'd kept the details of the two churches in central London that my Australian minister had recommended. So the following Sunday, armed with an address, I headed off to an evening service at one of them. This decision was to have a major impact on my life, and even today I can get somewhat overcome with gratitude as remember it.

It was a long journey by public transport from the southwest of London into the city. I caught the tube to Oxford Circus, walked up Regent Street, and there it was: All Souls, Langham Place, the church made famous by the ministry of John Stott. Like the church I'd visited the previous Sunday, All Souls was an old traditional building, but it had been freshened up on the inside. I only caught the last ten minutes of the service, but the congregation was large and diverse, the music was engaging, and from my minister's recommendation I knew that the teaching would be good. This was the sort of place I understood. I asked about Bible study groups and discovered that they had a mid-week group, the All Souls International Fellowship group (ASIF), for overseas visitors who were in London for anything from a few weeks to a few years. It sounded like just the thing for me, and I decided to join. After a few weeks without fellowship, it was really great to be among God's people again, and I remained part of this church and the ASIF group for the rest of my stay.

Good churches that seek to teach and apply the Scriptures are absolute gold. In some places it may take time and effort to find one, and you may need to expend a fair amount of energy to get to it from where you're staying. Yet this is time, effort and energy well spent. At All Souls and in the ASIF group I heard God's word explained and discussed, I prayed with others, I experienced fellowship (Acts 2:42) and I was spurred on toward love and good deeds (Heb 10:24). My time there stimulated my reading of and reflections on God's word, it motivated me to pray, and it encouraged me to rely upon and apply scriptural truths in what was then to me a somewhat alien environment. God used this extended and intensive involvement to shape me into a more Christlike person than I'd previously been.

That first trip to London was the only time I stayed in one place overseas long enough to put down any roots in a church. My other trips have been shorter and have involved more moving around, but I've enjoyed visiting churches and meeting with God's people in England, the United States, Wales, India, Thailand, Bali, Kenya, Uganda, South Africa and Malawi. I have heard good sermons, experienced Christian hospitality, learned how God is working in the lives of different people and in different places, and been motivated to keep putting Christ first in my life. Meeting with believers from other countries and cultural backgrounds has done my relationship with God the world of good. I hope that, in some way, God has also used me to encourage them.

Time to think

Being utterly alone in the middle of nowhere was strangely invigorating. I'd walked out of the camping ground of the Matobo National Park in Zimbabwe and headed off down the road for a few kilometres. Ostensibly I was looking for a lift, but that would really only have required me to stand on the edge of the camping area with an expectant look and an outstretched finger. I think what I really wanted was to go out alone into Africa, and to feel it surround me.

I could see no other signs of life—only flat, grassy plains interspersed with granite-topped hills. It was just me, my pack, the ground, the rocks and the sky. Besides my flight out of the country in a few weeks' time, I had no commitments, nowhere I needed to be. I could have walked back to the campsite and spent more time there, or I could have headed in the other direction towards Bulawayo. In fact, had I been so inclined, I could have walked off into the grasslands and tried to survive in the wild.

Up until then, my 24 years of existence had been highly urbanized and scheduled—guided by my watch, by daily events, weekly commitments, the yearly calendar, life expectations. There had always been somewhere I needed to be, something I needed to be getting ready for, or someone who wanted me to do something. No longer was this the case. No-one was expecting me for a meal, there were no classes to attend or weekend sports to play, and no-one within a few thousand miles had any plans for me.[4] With the passage of the sun across the sky my watch seemed somewhat irrelevant. Here was life stripped bare, devoid of all its toys and distractions. Standing there on an open road that snaked through a timeless landscape, I reflected on the sheer emptiness. I was alone with God.

Being away from home and away from our normal routines and responsibilities can often prompt reflective thinking. I have found that it can provide the mental space to contemplate God, and to mull over the bigger issues that often get squeezed out in the rush and commotion of everyday living. Sustained time doing this kind of thinking can be something of a watershed experience. One lady from my church told me that she experienced a real turning point in her Christian faith while travelling around Europe in a van with her husband. "Being out of my normal daily life and finding myself with time to reflect was a real positive", she said. Another couple who travelled together for a few months told me that it was terrific for their marriage, as well as for thinking about their priorities and future direction. The husband said, "It removed the 'white noise' of ordinary life and gave us time to focus and think with greater clarity about life and what it should look like".

I strongly suggest taking a Christian book or two away with you, as you'll probably have more time to read than you do in your normal life back home. On my first trip I devoured

4 This was before the age of 24/7 connectivity!

various books to my very great benefit, including the famous Christian biography *God's Smuggler* and Billy Graham's *The Holy Spirit*. You may also like to take some Christian music with you. Songs often form the soundtracks of our lives, so why not put a few positive ones on the playlist?

Time to think combined with new sights, sounds and insights can also inspire creativity. In London, for example, my output of poetry spiked. In the small hours of one morning, I penned 'On watching a TV special about *The Velvet Underground* and how my reaction relates to the world situation in general' (and that was just the title!). This and most of the other poems I wrote while I was away were my reflections on life viewed through the lens of Scripture. Why not try some creative writing, journaling or even composing while on your travels?

'Christian' locations

Pilgrimages, or journeys to places that are linked in some way to a person's beliefs, are part of many religious traditions. Buddhists may visit Bodh Gaya in India—the place where the Buddha is said to have gained enlightenment. A pilgrimage to Mecca in Saudi Arabia is, in fact, mandatory for all Muslims who are financially and physically able. Of course, as Christians we know that no one part of God's world is holier or more spiritual than any other. When I talk about 'Christian' locations, I simply mean places where a significant Christian event took place, or is remembered. So, while I've never been on a pilgrimage (and, in fact, I see no biblical warrant for it), I have travelled to places that have enhanced my Christian reflection.

The first genuine biblical location I visited was Athens. In Acts 17, Luke describes how the apostle Paul visited this city and preached in the synagogue and marketplace. His teaching was such that it excited (or disturbed) the attention of some local philosophers, who had him brought to a meeting of the Areopagus—a city court or council concerned with various matters, including religious ones. Here, before this group of men, Paul again took the opportunity to preach. In one of the most significant speeches recorded in the New Testament, Paul introduced the gospel to his pagan hearers, after first establishing some common ground with them by responding to various aspects of their Greco-Roman culture. It is an exciting and much-studied speech, the result of which was that a few people became followers of Jesus: "Among them was Dionysius, a member of the Areopagus, also a woman named Damaris, and a number of others" (Acts 17:34).

I was keen to visit the hill in Athens called the Areopagus, where it's thought that Paul delivered his speech. So, one humid sunny Sunday afternoon, I walked across the city and up this hill. As the evening shadows lengthened, I pulled out my Bible and had myself photographed reading Acts 17 by some unsuspecting and somewhat confused Spanish tourist. Although I can't quite put my finger on why, there was something quite powerful about simply being where this significant event from the pages of the New Testament actually took place.

While I am perhaps more inspired by being in the great outdoors, I've sometimes found sitting in churches to be conducive to reflection as well. One misty afternoon I found myself in St Peter, a picturesque German village just outside of Freiburg, surrounded by the Black Forest and rolling hills.

It started to drizzle, so I sought refuge in a church. It was a beautiful old building and very peaceful inside, so I took the opportunity to think and pray. On the wall there was a picture of the crucified Christ, and another of the apostle Peter being crucified upside down. After his resurrection, Jesus had indeed warned Peter of what lay ahead:

> "Very truly I tell you, when you were younger you dressed yourself and went where you wanted; but when you are old you will stretch out your hands, and someone else will dress you and lead you where you do not want to go." (John 21:18)

Sitting there in these evocative surroundings, away from the normal routine of life, I was reminded that suffering and persecution are part of the Christian life and shouldn't take us by surprise.

Another site I found absolutely fascinating is one I visited in Haarlem, a large town about 15 minutes by train from Amsterdam. Anyone who knows me well knows that I have been inspired by a Dutch Christian woman named Corrie ten Boom. Corrie is one of my heroes. She was an unmarried, middle-aged watchmaker when the Nazis overran Holland during the Second World War. More significantly, she was a very keen Christian. As the occupation took hold, she and her family helped to smuggle Jewish people out of Europe and away from the Nazi holocaust. They constructed a small secret room in their house to hide both Jewish people and members of the Dutch resistance. They operated successfully for quite a long time before being betrayed to the Nazis in 1944 by one of their own countrymen. Corrie and her sister Betsie were sent to Ravensbrük, the notorious women's concentration camp in Germany. Despite the horrendous conditions, the two of them led services and Bible studies and were used by God to bring many people to the Lord.[5]

The house and watchmaker's shop where Corrie lived and worked still stands, and is now a museum. Much of the house has been preserved to look as it did in the 1940s. The hiding place—a small room behind a cupboard in Corrie's bedroom—can still be seen, along with photos of Corrie and Betsie and their father and many others.

As Betsie ten Boom lay dying in Ravensbrük near the end of 1944, she urged her sister, Corrie:

> [We] must tell people what we have learned here. We must tell them that there is no pit so deep that He is not deeper still. They will listen to us, Corrie, because we have been here.[6]

Corrie took these words to heart. After the war, she spent decades travelling the world and testifying to the work of God in her own life, in her sister's life, and in the lives of many others in that camp. And today the Corrie ten Boom House in Haarlem still testifies to God's goodness for all who have ears to hear.

Relying and applying

Being far from home and away from our normal support structures and coping mechanisms can encourage our

5 If you haven't already, I highly recommend reading her story in her book *The Hiding Place*, or watching the well-made movie by the same name.

6 Corrie ten Boom, *The Hiding Place*, Hodder & Stoughton, London, 1976, p. 202.

reliance on God. I've found this to be true on countless occasions, including those hours on the train stalled on the plains of Botswana. A girl from my church, who admits she had a fairly protected upbringing, told me she was a bit nervous when she first went travelling but that it made her "very reliant on God and prayerful".

Travelling and living abroad also provides a myriad of opportunities for *applying* God's word. John and Brad, the guys I mentioned earlier who went on a young adults' package tour of Europe, once had just such an opportunity. They were in Amsterdam, near the end of their trip, when the tour leader told the group, "When you're in Paris you go to the Eiffel Tower. When you're in Rome you go to the Colosseum. And when you're in Amsterdam you go to a sex show."

My two friends faced a dilemma. The entertainment planned for the evening clearly fell outside the parameters of appropriate Christian behaviour, yet the whole group was supposed to be going. Wisely, John and Brad had already made a conscious decision to live as Christians and to be public about their faith during their trip, and with mutual encouragement they had been spending daily time with God. As a result they were well equipped to rely on and apply the truths of God's word in this situation. When the plans for the night were announced, these two men firmly decided that they would not go. In fact, they went further and encouraged other group members not to go. The relationships they had built up during the trip were such that they got a good hearing. In the end, the tour leaders went to the sex show without anyone else from the tour group!

God's word tells us that there are things we should and shouldn't do, and a close relationship with him will help us to rely on and apply these truths as we travel or live abroad. As we've seen, for example, we should meditate on Scripture and pray regularly, encourage other believers, and point non-believers to Christ. Similarly, there are various things we're to avoid. Classic pitfalls to watch out for include sexual immorality, excessive alcohol consumption and illegal drug use.

Sexual immorality

As is the case in many parts of the world, travelling in South-East Asia provides many opportunities to indulge in numerous forms of sexual immorality. In some places, sex workers are everywhere. Taxi drivers offer to link you up with them and the workers themselves are often plying their trade openly on the streets. I was out walking one morning in Bangkok when a nice-looking young woman—someone who would not have looked out of place at church back home—walked up and politely offered me a particular sexual service. Had I been so inclined (which I wasn't), it would have been very easy to simply say yes, pay the relatively small sum of money, and slip into a nearby room.

Many sex shows in that city are described as must-see tourist attractions. One traveller I know, who did not attend one, told me that other travellers would say to him, "I want to go and see the show, but I want the girls to be well-treated". That would no doubt be the view of many people. As Christians, however, we need to see the fundamental disconnect between this attitude and propping up an industry that causes unimaginable harm to these women.

Sex workers and sex shows are obvious temptations to avoid, but the opportunity for sexual immorality can come in subtler forms as well. The line between a God-given blessing and a major moral mistake often comes down to whether or not we exercise godly obedience at a particular point.

I had checked into a youth hostel in Bulawayo when I met Claudia from Germany. In the hostel common room I fell into conversation with her and some Americans who were there to build mudbrick houses. Claudia was a medical student, which meant she was bright. She was in Africa, which meant she was interesting. And she was very attractive. Nothing wrong with any of this so far.

After dinner I put out a general invitation to anyone who wanted to go out for the evening. Two of the Americans agreed to come, as did Claudia. We spent the evening in happy conversation, and after an hour or two the Americans decided to head back to the hostel. Claudia and I were getting on very nicely and decided to stay on a bit longer. I don't think I'd mentioned my Christian faith at this point.

Eventually, we too decided that we should head back. So I found myself out walking on a moonlit night with a girl I liked. As we strolled along, it occurred to me that this could potentially go in a couple of directions. I had one of those 'two voices in the head' moments. Voice one: "You're in Zimbabwe. She's a stunner. She obviously likes you. No-one knows you're here. Of course you're not going to have sex with her, but why not have a little bit of fun? No-one ever needs to know." Voice two: "Stephen, you're a Christian. You've got this far without any major mistakes in this area of your life. Don't start now. Don't let God down. She's a nice girl—treat her well. Do the right thing!"

Thankfully, and no doubt in large part because I sought to travel with God, voice two won the day. Claudia asked me a question. I can't remember what it was, but it was something that required me to share my Christian beliefs in order to answer her sincerely. So on that moonlit night, walking along with this beautiful girl, I made the right choice. After a moment's hesitation, I told her that my Christian faith had a big impact on my answer to her question. As I began to explain, I realized that she was paying very close attention to what I was saying. "I've just become a Christian myself", she eventually blurted out. She'd been brought up as a 'cultural' Christian but had recently committed her life to Christ and was now attending a Baptist church. From there, our mutual enthusiasm for the conversation grew exponentially. Back at the hostel, we talked into the small hours of the morning. And to think that for a second or so I'd toyed with the idea of doing something really stupid! Claudia and I remained in contact for a year or two, and I still sometimes pray for her.

The apostle Paul writes to Timothy: "Treat younger men as brothers, older women as mothers, and younger women as sisters, with absolute purity" (1 Tim 5:1b-2). When we're travelling, we need to follow this excellent advice just as we do at home, and treat members of the opposite sex with "absolute purity". This is best for others, it's best for us, and it brings glory to God.

Alcohol and illegal drugs

A close relationship with God will help us apply God's word and make good decisions when it comes to drugs and alcohol as well. I've had some exposure overseas to the offer or availability of drugs but I've had far more contact with people engaging in excessive alcohol consumption, and I know this is the experience of many others as well. A friend who recently returned from South-East Asia told me that many of the travellers he met would drink heavily at night in the bars. Some told him they'd never do anything like that back home. Many people seem to think that different rules apply when you're overseas—that what happens overseas stays overseas.

The Scriptures tell us in various places to avoid getting drunk. See Ephesians 5 for just one example: "Do not get drunk on wine, which leads to debauchery. Instead, be filled with the Spirit" (Eph 5:18). So not getting drunk is an issue of obedience. We also know that inebriated people can cause great damage to others and to themselves, and are vulnerable because they're not thinking clearly. When we are away from home and from people we know and trust, why would we leave ourselves open to being taken advantage of in any number of ways?

Back when I was about 18, I decided that I would never have more than two alcoholic drinks on any one occasion. Over the years this decision has meant that I can be social in this way if I wish, set clear limits for myself, and retain self-control. You may like to set a similar limit for yourself. As I said earlier, I am 194 centimetres tall (6'4"), so if you're of a different size and constitution you may need to set a different limit to ensure that you remain in control of your actions. It might be helpful to have a wise Christian friend help you as you determine an appropriate limit in this area. Unfortunately, some people are unable to stick to predetermined limits when it comes to alcohol. If that is you then it's probably best for you to avoid drinking altogether.

Another thing to consider is whether our drinking is likely to tempt another person to drink too much—in which case it would be better for us to abstain. We need to be sensitive not only to our own limits but also to the temptations that others face.

My two-drink limit has proved to be very helpful on my overseas trips, especially during my time in London. The men in the cricket club had a wide range of approaches to alcohol consumption. In England, as in Australia, there were some who drank a lot. They would play cricket on Saturday and then drink into the night. They'd play cricket on Sunday and then drink into the night. As the evenings wore on, debates often raged over such critical matters as the relative merits of lager versus bitter. While I often had one or two drinks, I was not pushed beyond that, and I remained in good control of my behaviour. If I was still thirsty, there was always lemon squash.

Sadly, the combination of alcohol and sexual immorality is all too frequently seen. This was unappealingly exemplified for me on an overnight train trip in Zimbabwe between Victoria Falls and Bulawayo. I was in a cabin with a double-bunk. During the night the man who had the bottom bunk burst into the cabin, reeking of alcohol. "Hey, can I bring a girl in with me, mate?" he asked.

Still half asleep and not really comprehending what was happening, I think I mumbled something like, "Errr, sure". The next thing I knew, this guy and some girl (who was also very drunk) were on the bottom bunk engaging in… well, the sounds that drifted up from below could not have been a worse advertisement for a one-night stand. When they fell asleep, I lay awake breathing in the alcoholic fumes and listening to some of the loudest snoring I have ever heard. It was a depressing scene.

Remain in the vine! Travelling closely with God is best for us and for others and enables us to glorify God. When we travel with God we're able not only to avoid making bad decisions but also to have a positive impact on people we meet.

Checklist for travelling with God

- Resolve to travel with God.
- Resolve to live as a Christian while away, relying upon and applying God's word.
- Prioritize spending time with God, and plan ahead—what you'll read, how you'll order your prayer time, and when you might schedule your daily time with God.
- Consider taking some Christian books and music with you.
- Prioritize tracking down good Christian fellowship. Join a church if you're in any one location for an extended period of time, and get involved.
- Make the most of opportunities for reflection and visiting 'Christian' locations.
- Be prepared to resist temptations relating to sexual immorality, excessive alcohol consumption, and illegal drugs.
- Expect that you will be tempted to do *none* of the things suggested in this checklist. Don't let sin ruin your time abroad—or your life.

2

TRAVELLING GOD'S WORLD

For the Lord *is the great God,*
the great King above all gods.
In his hand are the depths of the earth,
and the mountain peaks belong to him.
The sea is his, for he made it,
and his hands formed the dry land.
Come, let us bow down in worship,
let us kneel before the Lord *our Maker…* (Ps 95:3-6)

My senses were in overdrive as I walked off the plane and into the terminal. It was crowded and noisy, and the sights, sounds and smells were quite unlike those I'd left behind in Sydney. As my fellow passengers dispersed into the crowd, I became increasingly aware of my skin's lack of pigmentation. It was my first time in Africa, and I had never felt so white.

Thanks to some pre-departure planning, a friend of a friend—a European Zimbabwean by the name of Greg—

picked me up from the arrivals area at Harare International Airport. He probably identified me in the crowd by my bewildered expression. That night he kindly accommodated me in a house that could very well have been a Sydney residence, except for the bars on the windows and the security guard out front.

The following morning Greg dropped me off in the city centre, where I was to meet two Australian friends I was going to travel with for a few days. Arriving early, I was once again extremely conscious of my white skin. I felt as though everyone was staring at me. I bought a newspaper and studied the world both on and off the page. On the page, I read about a government minister resigning over a perjury charge, and noticed that people were often referred to as 'Cde'—short for 'Comrade'. This was the world of Robert Mugabe. Off the page, I noticed the great variety of people, along with examples of the world's unequal distribution of wealth. Some people asked me for money. Others offered me wood carvings and money-changing services.

Culture shock is the disorientation a person feels when entering a new country with an unfamiliar way of life. I was clearly experiencing it to some degree. While I was sort of enjoying myself, it was in a cautious, tense sort of way. Eventually my two friends showed up, and the feelings of discomfort eased.

Just after sunrise the following morning, the three of us arrived at the city bus station to catch the bus to Kariba, in the north of the country. The air was brisk and the bus station packed. Apart from some other backpackers, we were the only white-skinned people in sight. The bus took us through flat farmland and fields of wheat, tobacco and cattle. We saw gum trees (like those in Australia) but also some short, dense vegetation and round houses with thatched roofs that gave the landscape a distinctively African appearance. When we entered a town the bus would bypass the more affluent sections and pull into colourful, noisy bus station and market areas, where we'd be surrounded immediately by people selling oranges, bananas, hard-boiled eggs, bread rolls and ice-cream.

When we reached Kariba we checked into a campground on the edge of Lake Kariba, the world's largest human-made lake, which was formed by damming the waters of the powerful Zambezi River. We pitched our tent and then walked back into town. It was a Sunday afternoon and many people were gathered in the square near the shops. Here we witnessed a very curious sight.

Men dressed in priestly robes with crosses on them were dancing in a frenzied fashion to loud bongo and maraca music. Sometimes they would stop and someone would speak before the dancing and music started up again. A local told us that it was the Zion Church. I didn't know what to make of it, as the speech was not in English. It looked to me like traditional African dancing and music applied to Christianity. I learned later that there are many Christian denominations unique to Africa that span the entire spectrum—from thoroughly biblical groups to dangerous cults.

The next day on a sun-drenched ferry trip along Lake Kariba we saw elephants, buffalo, warthog and deer, and a magnificent orange sunset. We met a family from South Africa who had links with African Enterprise—a Christian ministry with which I would have much to do in years to come.

The next morning, we caught a lift to the town of Victoria Falls. The settlement is about a kilometre from the falls, but even from that distance you are very much aware of them. You can hear the sound of distant thunder and there's a permanent cloud of mist on the horizon. As you move closer the rumble grows louder and the mist reveals itself as spray. With all the water in the air, the vegetation has morphed from the semi-arid into rainforest. A lush jungle exists where all else around is dry and dusty.

Sodden but expectant we walked through the forest into a clearing, and there it was: Mosi-oa-Tunya—'the smoke that thunders'. The waters of the mighty Zambezi River plunge over a hundred-metre cliff almost two kilometres wide, its spray drenching everything in its vicinity. Victoria Falls is one of the most awe-inspiring sights I've ever seen. Its vast magnificence is utterly captivating. I could not take my eyes off it. Over the next few days I went back again and again, to see the falls from different locations and at different times. One afternoon, double rainbows appeared in the spray. It was as if the glories of heaven had descended upon this patch of the earth. Surely even an atheist would be moved to consider the existence of a creative, supernatural force when face-to-face with such a vision.

Africa had gotten under my skin.

This is God's world

The world is an amazing place. It should be—it is God's world. The book of Genesis tells us that God made the world and everything in it, all from nothing. He made the light and the darkness; the earth, sun, moon and stars; the water, land and sky; the plants, birds, fish and animals; and the human race. And at the end of his work, "God saw all that he had made, and it was very good" (Gen 1:31).

Of course, as Genesis 3 tells us, the creation has been marred by human sin. But like a ruined masterpiece, it still retains much of its glory. Psalm 95 reminds us that the impressive nature of God's creation should drive us to worship God:

> In his hand are the depths of the earth,
>   and the mountain peaks belong to him.
> The sea is his, for he made it,
>   and his hands formed the dry land.
> Come, let us bow down in worship,
>   let us kneel before the Lord our Maker (vv. 4-6)

Travelling and living overseas provides opportunities to meet incredible people, learn about intriguing cultures, and witness some of the breathtaking wonders of creation. When we view all of this through the lens of Scripture and with the enlightening power of the Holy Spirit, we appreciate more and more that we're travelling God's world.

The people

When you ask someone who has returned from abroad to tell you what they liked best about their time away, more often than not they'll say, "It was the people!" Beautiful sights can be memorable, cultures can be enriching, food can be palate-stretching and experiences can be mind-blowing, but the people we meet often make or break our time away.

This shouldn't surprise us. The Scriptures tell us that God created human beings in his own image as the pinnacle of creation:

> So God created mankind in his own image,
> in the image of God he created them;
> male and female he created them. (Gen 1:27)

Furthermore, God loves people so much that his own Son, Jesus, died on the cross for them:

> For God so loved the world that he gave his one and only Son, that whoever believes in him shall not perish but have eternal life. (John 3:16)

Everyone you meet overseas—whether local, expat or fellow traveller—is important to God.

You will really click with many of the people you meet, and you may stay in contact with some of them for many years. Some will be Christians, others won't, but each has the capacity to enrich your life, and you in turn have the opportunity to enrich theirs. You will also meet people who are so utterly different from you that you'll struggle to relate to them. They may annoy you or seem selfish, not be 'your sort of person', and perhaps even have attitudes you find repugnant. You might be tempted to be rude or to exclude them, or to hold them in contempt. But God created them, and Jesus died to offer them the same forgiveness he offers you.

The most helpful thing we can do for people we meet is to encourage those who are Christians, and to point those who are not towards Jesus. I always pray when I travel that God will give me both sorts of opportunities, and God has answered those prayers many times (but more about that in the next two chapters).

Meeting the locals

When visiting or living in another country, it's great to meet and get to know the people who actually live there. It's a shame if we only interact with locals in their roles as bus driver, shopkeeper, tour guide or hostel worker. Meeting local residents is much easier, of course, if you're working in the country. But if you aren't working, there are a few ways to maximize your chances of meeting locals: seeking out contacts, finding people with common interests, and using public transport.

Contacts

Before my first trip overseas, friends and family members gave me the names and contact details of people they knew. Perhaps the most memorable of these was Olive. Many years before, when my mother was a young girl, this older, very distant relative visited Australia. Olive and my mother struck up a friendship and corresponded for decades, so my mother was very keen for me to visit her while I was in England. Accordingly, a few months into my trip I caught the train to Bristol to meet Olive, who was then in her mid-eighties.

She picked me up in a zippy little car and we drove, chatting all the way, through the Cotswolds to Stratford-upon-Avon, where she'd booked us into a hotel. She had organized for me to attend the Royal Shakespeare Company's performance of *Romeo and Juliet* that night. The following day she drove us through Gloucester to the Forest of Dean, where we had a nice pub lunch (the sort one can only have in an English country pub) before driving to her home in Yate for afternoon tea. She served me a home-cooked meal that night and we looked through old family photos. She was one of the coolest 80-year-olds I've ever met.

These kinds of connections with relatives, friends, friends of friends, and even random people we meet along the way can be fun and can also give us insights into the culture of another country. But a word of caution here—it is important to make sure that we are giving to the other person, not simply using them. And it is always good to avoid outstaying our welcome, particularly if they're generous enough to provide us with a bed.

Common interests

Another great way to meet locals is to find people who share your interests. Your pastime may be quilting or stamps or rugby; or perhaps you belong to your local fireman's association. Before leaving home, see if you can track down and make contact with people or groups in the country you'll be visiting who share your interest. On my first trip it was a cinch—I had the cricket club and I joined a church.

Through the club, I met and socialized with Londoners. I got to know them, got a sense of what it was like to live in London, and got to do the sorts of things that Londoners normally did. Life at the cricket club was endlessly informative and entertaining, and I will be forever grateful for the warmth and hospitality shown by so many of the people I met there. They truly gave me an insight into life in England.

Public transport

Catching public transport, particularly long-distance public transport, is another great way to meet locals. One Friday in

Zimbabwe I decided that the time had come to visit the Great Zimbabwe Ruins—impressive rock structures that are the remains of a city that flourished between 500 and 1000 years ago. It's one of the most important archaeological sites in Africa, and perhaps the most impressive one south of the Sahara.

On the bus trip I fell into conversation with a local guy, a school teacher called Wellington. As time passed and our conversation got more personal, he shared various philosophical viewpoints with me. "All change except fools and prophets", he told me. "If we share something, you become my brother. If you can't share anything material, you can share your mind."

When the bus stopped in a village for lunch, Wellington invited me into a tin shed to share a meal that seemed to have been put on predominantly for employees of the bus company. The lunch included sudza (a little like mashed potato) with stew, which was served in a large common metal bowl and eaten with one's fingers. A dozen or more men dug eagerly into the bowl. The shed was far from clean, AIDS was rife in the country, and the chance of an accidental exchange of saliva was certainly on the cards—so a communal stew was the last thing I felt like eating. But everyone was so clearly going out of their way to make this stranger from a foreign country feel at home that I didn't want to disappoint. "Dear God, please don't let me catch anything", I prayed silently as I tucked into a polite amount of stew.

My conversation with Wellington continued after lunch. At one point his theme changed and, given the history of his country, his comments were striking. "To hate is inhuman", he said. "To hate is insanity. War is like a storm." Admittedly he smoked and drank most of the way, but he was very friendly and I learned a lot that day from his conversation and his hospitality.

Be friendly and flexible

Many years later, when I was heading back to Africa to do some short-term theological lecturing, I sought out a former missionary to that part of the world for some advice. "Be kind", he urged. "If you're kind to people, they are more likely to forgive you your cultural misunderstandings". It was good advice, and can obviously be applied anywhere in the world. Seek to be friendly and kind when you meet people.

Flexibility is also important. People in other cultures don't necessarily do things the way we do at home. I once travelled to India, for example, with the then Anglican Archbishop of Sydney and his wife (as one does!). The fact that I was in India with an archbishop meant that I was treated with a level of hospitality far beyond anything I felt I deserved. When we were invited out for meals, the women prepared the food but did not join the men when we sat down to eat. Instead they continued to wait on us, eating separately once we had finished. I found this disconcerting, but I realized that this was their custom and I needed to accept their hospitality graciously.

Sometimes I've found certain cultural practices harder to accept—especially when I've witnessed racism. In one country, I found the attitudes of some Westerners towards the local population to be fairly disturbing. In these circumstances I did my best to model respectful cross-cultural interaction.

Communication can be another challenge. Language differences are an obvious barrier, but body language customs can also vary enormously across cultures. During that trip to India, I gave a children's talk to about 600 children. The day before the talk I practised what I was going to say with a local Christian leader to make sure that the way I presented my content was culturally appropriate. As I went through the talk, he just sat there shaking his head. There were obviously a few problems. The more I spoke, the more he shook his head. It looked like this really was not going that well. When I finished, to my great surprise he said, "That's great!" Head-shaking in his culture apparently means 'I'm listening' or 'Okay'. This taught me to make fewer assumptions about cultures different from my own.

Meeting other travellers

One of the joys of the road is meeting other travellers—people from other places who are travelling in the same direction. I've formed some great friendships this way, some of which remain to this day.

Sometimes you'll meet someone (or a group of people) with whom you get on really well, but your schedule or plans mean that you spend only a day or two together. Someone has said of backpacking, "You meet someone, become great friends for a few days and then say goodbye, never to see them again". That certainly can be true, but as Christians hopefully we have left them with something to think about, and we can continue to pray for them for many years.

One of the downsides of travelling on your own is going for extended periods without meeting anyone with whom you can share your experiences. I had one pretty quiet spell travelling through Eastern Europe. I was doing and seeing remarkable things, but there was no-one with whom to share any of it. The lone traveller needs to be able to cope with extended periods in his or her own company.

If you want to meet other travellers, there are a few ways to maximize your chances: staying in accommodation where other travellers are staying, using public transport, and going on organized tours.

Accommodation

Every city has hostels and other low-cost accommodation options that offer backpackers and other budget-conscious travellers a decent place to stay, as well as camaraderie and a friendly atmosphere. Returning from Europe on one occasion I decided to stop in Bangkok for a few days. As always, I was keen to meet people. I caught a taxi from the airport and asked to be dropped off on the Khao San Road, which was where I was told all the backpackers went.[7] I found some budget accommodation, and over dinner I struck up a conversation with a fellow Australian—Simon, a carpenter from Sydney. He had also just arrived, and we spent the next couple of days exploring the city and resisting the scams habitually foisted on foreign tourists.

Public transport

As with meeting locals, using public transport is a great way to meet other travellers. Those few days in Bangkok had given

7 If you've ever read Alex Garland's book *The Beach* (or seen the movie of the same name), you'll understand when I say that my first few hours in Bangkok had a lot in common with those of the story's main character.

me a taste for Asia, so during my second year at theological college I visited Thailand and Laos on a 13-day budget holiday with Bruce, a fellow student. One of the highlights of the trip proved to be catching the slow boat down the Mekong River from Chiang Khong in Thailand to Luang Prabang in Laos. It was a two-day journey by public transport.

There were about 20 backpackers on the boat, as well as seven locals plus the crew. The first day saw us take a six-hour trip to Pak Beng through a forested mountainous region with a smattering of villages and a wild elephant or two on the riverside. The views were great, but it was the experience *on* the boat that made the trip memorable. The happy throng included people from England, Scotland, Ireland, Sweden, France and Australia, and we talked and laughed throughout the trip, and ate together the first night at Pak Beng and again the following night in Luang Prabang. Three members of the group arrived in Sydney in the following months, and Bruce and I were able to show them some Australian hospitality.

Tours

Tours are, of course, another good way to meet fellow travellers. I've never been on an extended tour, but in various places I've done short tours ranging from one to three days. Tours provide a ready-made group with whom to share your experiences.

Be friendly and flexible

Once again, it is good to have a friendly and flexible attitude when approaching other travellers. Many may be grateful for some companionship but too nervous (or cool) to make the first move, so when you stretch out the hand of friendship you'll often get many takers. Others may not be interested in spending time with you, so be ready for rebuffs. Remember, as a Christian your significance is found in Christ, and not in being popular with other people.

The natural world

As well as meeting lots of people on your travels, you'll see some fantastic examples of God's creative handiwork in the natural world:

> "You alone are the Lord. You made the heavens, even the highest heavens, and all their starry host, the earth and all that is on it, the seas and all that is in them. You give life to everything, and the multitudes of heaven worship you." (Neh 9:6)

In terms of jaw-dropping, postcard-worthy splendour, Victoria Falls stands out for me. But a few train journeys I took through Norway also live large in my memory. One September morning I left Oslo Central Station on a train heading west towards Bergen. Wooded hills and lakes gave way to a landscape of rock and snow as we gained altitude. On its journey over what is known as the 'Roof of Norway', the train passed through numerous tunnels designed to keep the snow off the tracks in particularly treacherous sections. I got off at a small mountaintop junction called Myrdal, where a few buildings clung tenaciously to a barren landscape of low vegetation, rocks and snowdrifts. Changing trains, I descended 863 metres to Flåm, a small town located far below at the inner end of the Aurlandsfjord. From here you could look up at the sides of the steep green valley plunging down into the blue-grey waters of the fjord. The whole scene was one of majestic space and splendour. Back at Myrdal, I sat on a rock next to a waterfall overlooking the cavernous valley and reflected, prayed, and penned some thoughts that I later turned to poetry.

That evening I returned to Oslo and then caught a night train that was heading north for the town of Bodø on the Norwegian coast. We sped past forests, fjords, lakes and mountains towards the alien beauty of the tundra north of the Arctic Circle. As we approached the arctic latitudes, with the autumn sun skirting the horizon and bathing everything with orange light that cast strange shadows, I found it hard to register that I was on the same planet as Sydney. This stunning landscape, like so many others, testifies to God's creativity and majesty.

If you spend most of your time in urban areas, as I do, you can lose touch with the wonder of the natural world. A good BBC nature documentary narrated by David Attenborough can lift you from your surroundings, but few things beat being out in the forests, deserts, mountain ranges and plains yourself. It really can help you to appreciate the wonder and complexity of the world God has created.

The wildlife

The writer of Proverbs 30 is clearly filled with admiration for our planet's wildlife. He speaks in awestruck tones of "a lion, mighty among beasts, who retreats before nothing" (v. 30), of "the way of an eagle in the sky" and "the way of a snake on a rock" (v. 19a). Having observed some of the world's most impressive animals in various African game parks, I can understand his awe.

In recent years I've had the opportunity to do regular short-term theological lecturing in Sub-Saharan Africa. During these trips I often take a couple of extra days to go sightseeing, and one of my favourite things is to visit game parks to see the wildlife. Three of my favourite parks are the Masai Mara National Reserve in Kenya, the South Luangwa National Park in Zambia, and the Bwindi Impenetrable National Park in Uganda. I've seen the 'Big Five'—lion, elephant, buffalo, leopard and rhinoceros—and can really appreciate why each of these magnificent animals is on that list.

Take the elephant, for example. Despite its massive bulk, fearsome tusks, dextrous trunk, floppy ears and pillar-like legs, it pads quietly through the land (unless provoked). I first saw elephants in the wild on the distant shores of Lake Kariba, but I had a much closer encounter a few days later. Peddling happily during a bike ride along the banks of the Zambezi River just above Victoria Falls, I rounded a corner and found myself face to face with a very large elephant. As I froze in my tracks, three thoughts crossed my mind:

1. This animal is not behind bars.
2. I can't change channels.
3. I can't pinch myself and wake up.

I looked at the elephant. The elephant looked at me. Ever so slowly, I backed my bike away. Once I'd successfully retreated around a corner, I turned the bike around and, peddling as hard as I could, put as much distance as possible between me and the elephant. Clearly I lived to tell the tale!

I find it sobering that different people can look at the same scene and draw completely different conclusions. When I see the double rainbows in Victoria Falls or the coiled power of a leopard, I think of the power and beauty of God's creation and I give glory to God. Someone who doesn't believe in God may look at the falls or the leopard and worship creation itself, rather than its creator. This has been a human tendency for thousands of years. As Romans 1 says:

> They [people] exchanged the truth about God for a lie, and worshiped and served created things rather than the Creator—who is forever praised. (v. 25)

Similarly, a Christian may look at the falls or the leopard and think of all the ways in which God has shaped and sustained them to this day. Paul writes:

> For in him [the Son] all things were created: things in heaven and on earth, visible and invisible, whether thrones or powers or rulers or authorities; all things have been created through him and for him. He is before all things, and in him all things hold together. (Col 1:16-17)

Thanks to scientific investigation, we now understand some of the detail of how God works in the world. An atheist, however, will look at the falls and the leopard and think only of the 'natural laws' that science has discovered, without seeing any greater power behind them.

Works of humanity

While the natural world is inspiring, the skills God has given to human beings in areas such as technology, trades, academia, sport and the arts have also resulted in some captivating sights and sounds. Way back in Genesis 4, we read that Jubal "was the father of all who play stringed instruments and pipes" (v. 21). In Exodus we learn that when the tabernacle was being built, God filled Bezalel "with wisdom, with understanding, with knowledge and with all kinds of skills—to make artistic designs for work in gold, silver and bronze, to cut and set stones, to work in wood and to engage in all kinds of artistic crafts" (Exod 35:31-33). And God has been filling people with these gifts of skill, strength, creativity and knowledge ever since. As a consequence the world is full of impressive cities, architectural edifices, galleries, concert halls, theatres, sporting arenas and restaurants.

The UK and Europe abound with beautiful castles and churches. I think my favourite castle would have to be Neuschwanstein Castle in Germany. Built in the 19th century by King Ludwig II of Bavaria in honour of the German composer Richard Wagner, it is better known these days as the castle that inspired Disneyland's famous Sleeping Beauty Castle The palace is situated at the foot of the Bavarian Alps, and is impressive from every angle. Ludwig is said to have been a little mad, but they say there's a fine line between madness and brilliance. He only managed to finish a few rooms, but what he completed is wonderfully ornate—and the view from the men's bathroom, looking out into the Alps towards the neighbouring castle of Hohenschwangau, must rank as one of the most impressive views from a men's urinal on the planet! Neuschwanstein is a real-life fairytale castle, and a testimony to the creative potential God gives to humanity.

The world's galleries and museums are brimming with countless and diverse examples of this God-given creative potential, with the Louvre in Paris ranking as one of the best museums in the world. It is perhaps best known as the home of Leonardo da Vinci's *Mona Lisa*. A friend once told me that when he visited the Louvre he saw a man with a video camera walk into the room in which the *Mona Lisa* hangs. He was filming as he entered, he filmed the entire time he was there, and he was still filming as he left. The camera didn't leave his face, so he didn't actually *see* the *Mona Lisa*. Now there's a lesson in how *not* to travel!

The Louvre is also home to important ancient history collections, and features exhibits from the empires of both the Old and New Testaments—Egypt, Assyria, Babylon and Rome—that bring the world of the Bible alive.

While I particularly love London and Paris, I also have a great fondness for the city of Prague. I finally got there with my wife on a post-marriage pre-children trip overseas. I'd wanted to go for years, ever since my first attempt was unsuccessful thanks to some Czech border guards kicking me off an overnight train from Poland. The guards had woken me at midnight to look at my documents. Apparently there was a problem with my visa, and before I knew it I found myself dumped at a remote rural station in the frozen Polish countryside. As I recall, the name of the village (which seemed to consist only of the station) consisted of the letter Z followed by pretty much every other letter in the alphabet. I had no choice but to spread out my sleeping bag on a bench, put on as many clothes as possible, and get in. When I say it was freezing, I mean it was *freezing*. During the night pretty much every item from my backpack ended up in my sleeping bag with me. And I still froze!

There was no such drama years later when my wife and I arrived in Prague. We stayed three nights in the Old Town section of the city, exploring the square, the city hall with its astronomical clock, the Jewish quarter, and many wonderful old church buildings. All this is just across the river and down the hill from Prague Castle and the breathtaking St Vitus Cathedral.

As culturally and architecturally rich as Prague is, however, there is also a sad side to it. While many of the churches host excellent concerts, there is little evidence of any active church life. After enjoying an evening of classical music in one church building, I looked around the walls and noticeboards for any signs of Christian ministry. Nothing. This wonderful city struck me as somewhat godless.

So I was encouraged during our brief time there to experience two (admittedly minor) brushes with believers. At the Old Town Square one day I was standing near a statue of Jan Hus, the early Christian Reformer, and before I realized what had happened a man had slipped a Christian tract into my hand. At a hostel a few days later, we saw a note pinned to a noticeboard inviting people to a Bible study. I've prayed since that these kinds of efforts in Prague are bearing fruit. Europe is one of the many places in the world badly in need of prayer and Christian mission.

The marks that human beings have left on the world can be horribly depressing, but our creations can also be utterly inspiring. As Christians, we need to thank God for the abilities he's given to humanity. By his common grace God distributes gifts and talents among Christian and non-Christian alike for the good order and enjoyment of society. So we can thank God for da Vinci paintings and fairytale palaces, even when the creators are not believers.

Culture shock

There is, of course, a potential downside to travelling God's world and experiencing new cultures: culture shock. It can manifest as feelings of stress, disorientation, confusion, fear or anger, and travellers should be ready for it, particularly when first entering a country that is very different from their own.[8]

I didn't experience culture shock when I went to the UK or to Europe, but I was certainly on edge for my first few days in both Africa and Asia. In Africa, for example, I had the feeling that everyone was staring at me and that people were looking for an opportunity to rip me off. It was about a week before I felt fairly comfortable walking around, catching public transport, shopping and relating to people. From what other travellers have told me, I would say my experience of mild culture shock is fairly standard. Prayer can help here, as well as learning a bit about the country before your arrival.

I believe it is different if you travel to a very different

8 Paul G Hiebert, *Anthropological Insights for Missionaries*, Baker, Grand Rapids, 1985, pp. 64-74.

culture for an extended period of time. You might progress through the following stages: the *tourist stage* (when everything is new, fascinating and exciting), *disenchantment* (when the cultural differences lead to frustrations and anxiety), *resolution* (e.g. when you start to deal with the stresses through humour and sympathy) and *adjustment* (when you start to feel comfortable in the new culture). People sometimes also experience *reverse* culture shock when they return to their country and culture of origin because they have changed, and things with which they were once familiar may now cause irritation or frustration.[9] If you are moving to a very different cultural context for an extended period of time, it's worth reading up on how best to prepare.

The unexpected

Travelling overseas often brings with it the joy of unexpected experiences in God's world. New places always provide new people to meet, new sights to see and new things to experience. Some of these are life-changing; others are simply quirky. The most life-changing aspect of my travels was the international Christian fellowship I experienced at All Souls in London, but I will talk more about that in the next chapter. In the meantime, how about something quirky?

It was a sunny August morning when I arrived at the edge of the Okavango Delta, one of Africa's natural wonders. I booked into a lodge and paid for a two-day trip into the delta, leaving the following morning. A boat would take me into the swamps, where a local guide would show me around in a

9 Hiebert, pp. 74-80.

canoe for a few hours that afternoon and again the following morning. In between, I'd camp for the night on an island in the delta. At the end of my time with the guide on the second day, a boat would pick me up and return me to the lodge.

Sure enough, the next day I was taken by motor boat in through reedy marshes teeming with birdlife, and dropped on an island next to the Moremi Game Reserve. The island was roughly the size of a few football fields, and I had it all to myself. That afternoon, a local guide poled me around the waterways in a dugout canoe. The swamp was full at this particular time of year, making it better for birds than for game. So although I saw feathered life in abundance, the closest I got to any game was the splash of a hippopotamus. Back at the island for the night, I cooked myself some dinner and went to sleep in my tent.

The next morning as we poled through the waterways for another three hours, I saw impala, wildebeest and hippopotamus footprints. My guide dropped me back at the island to catch the boat back to the lodge, but it was 15 minutes *after* the boat had departed. The next return boat wasn't until the following day, and I'd used up all my tour-guided time, so it looked like I was going to be alone on an island in the middle of the Okavango Delta for 24 hours. Pretty much all I had with me was my tent, a little bit of food, and my Bible. What was I to do with all that time?

It's not often that one has a full day by oneself on a remote, swamp-enclosed African island with next to nothing. This was before the era of mobile phones, so I was absolutely alone with very little source of distraction. Time slowed down. It felt very basic and primal. I made some tea and soup. I read my Bible and prayed. I walked around the island

and made sure I wasn't sharing it with any wild animals. I thought a bit more. I watched the sun move across the sky, the shadows on the ground moving and getting longer. More prayer and contemplation. More soup and tea and a bit of bread. After dark, I walked to the centre of the island and looked up at the full moon and the stars.

If you are absolutely alone on an island, in warm weather and you are under a full moon, a number of ideas might occur to you. For example, you *might* think about removing your clothes and running around naked in the moonlight. And you might actually do it. Who can say?

I met the boat the next day and returned to my lodge, but that unexpected day on the island remains one of my fondest travel memories. That day I experienced life at its most basic: God, me, a bit of food, a Bible, and an island.

These stories show God's awe-inspiring creative work, as well as his care for us as we travel in his world.

Checklist for travelling God's world

- Resolve to travel with God.
- Remember that you're travelling and living in God's world.
- Praise and thank God for the incredible natural world that he's created—landscapes, plants and wildlife.
- Praise and thank God for creating humanity in all its diversity and giftedness.
- Remember that each person you meet is valuable to God.
- Be kind and flexible in your interactions with others.
- Expect that you will be tempted to do *none* of the things suggested in this checklist. Don't let sin ruin your time abroad—or your life.

3

CONNECTING WITH CHRISTIANS

And let us consider how we may spur one another on toward love and good deeds, not giving up meeting together, as some are in the habit of doing, but encouraging one another—and all the more as you see the Day approaching. (Heb 10:24-25)

About three hours by bus north-west of Athens is Delphi, one of Greece's premier travel destinations. Delphi sits atop a spur of Mount Parnassus, offering spectacular views of the Pleistos Valley. The Gulf of Corinth is also visible in the distance between the hills, but the scenery is not the main thing that attracts visitors to Delphi. In a country of archaeological abundance, Delphi is one of the premier sites. In particular, it is the location of the ruins of the Temple of Apollo—the site of the famous Oracle of Delphi.

I had just landed in Athens, and my initial impression of

the Greek capital was that it was hot, busy, and full of television aerials. Delphi took my fancy with its promise of a cooler climate and less congestion, so I caught a bus up into the hills. It was a pleasant drive on a cloudless day, past mountainside villages and olive groves.

I booked into a hostel, went for a quick wander around, and then retired to a nearby restaurant. I had a drink, read my Bible, prayed, and took in the magnificent views from the restaurant's veranda. While I was sitting there I met Jackie from South Africa and Alastair from England. We got on very nicely and ended up having dinner together, talking long into the twilight.

The following morning I was eating breakfast at the same restaurant, when Alastair joined me. "I saw you reading your Bible yesterday evening", he said. I nodded and explained that I was a Christian. He told me that he was, too, but he'd become a bit disillusioned. The good news was that he was thinking about recommitting himself to God. We had a bit of a chat and I did my best to encourage him before we parted ways. No doubt many people and situations had an impact on Alastair's spiritual walk over a number of years, and our encounter would only have played a very minor role. Still, it was gratifying that God had seen fit to use me as a small link in this man's spiritual chain.

This sort of meeting with another believer is far from unique. Travel can be full of such encounters.

Encouraging encounters

Meeting and spending time with other Christians is one of the most encouraging, motivating, productive and enjoyable things we can do in life—or, at least, it has the potential to be. When I've been away from home I've always been very keen to befriend and meet with other believers. One of my regular prayers while travelling has been that God would lead me to other believers I could encourage, and to non-believers to whom I could be a Christian witness. God has answered these prayers time and time again.

There are lots of things you can do to make sure that you meet other Christians as you're travelling. As I mentioned in the previous chapter, you can join a church if you're in one place for a period of time, or you can make a one-off visit to a church if you're simply passing through somewhere on a Sunday. You can also touch base with missionaries, link up with Christian organizations, and drop in on Christian relatives and friends. And then there are the many unplanned meetings with other believers—fellow travellers, expats or locals—whom God brings our way.

Whenever we meet other Christians, we should be aiming to have positive encounters. Unfortunately, it's possible to meet another believer and end up *dis*couraging them—in which case it would probably have been better that our paths had never crossed. On the other hand, a positive interaction may be the beginning (or continuation) of an ongoing relationship that we foster in some way or another.

As we'll see throughout this chapter, travelling and living overseas allows us to be part of God's worldwide purposes in a very personal way.[10]

10 Of course, you don't *need* to travel to be part of God's worldwide purposes. God can use us to have an international impact (in addition to our local impact) without us ever leaving home—through, for example, our prayers, our financial support of overseas ministry and aid, and our hospitality to foreign visitors.

Joining a church

During the week after my first Sunday at All Souls in London, I went to my first ASIF (All Souls International Fellowship) meeting. The small flat was jam-packed with people in their twenties and thirties from all over the world—Australians, Malaysians, Danes, Norwegians, and others from pretty much every continent. We all crushed into the modest living room, covering every available inch of floor space and even spilling out into the hallway. The leader of the group, to my slight surprise, was a short bespectacled grey-haired lady from Northern Ireland, called Eva. She had spent much of her life as a missionary in Japan but was now in her sixties or seventies and 'retired'.

I was used to church fellowship groups that met in large halls with cool 20- to 30-year-olds leading. But here we all were in a small private home, being hosted by a diminutive retiree with an infectious smile. But no-one seemed to care. Eva was like everyone's mother or grandmother, and perhaps because we were a long way from home this was just what we needed. We sang, listened to a talk, shared, prayed, and finished with tea. Paul writes in Galatians:

> So in Christ Jesus you are all children of God through faith, for all of you who were baptized into Christ have clothed yourselves with Christ. There is neither Jew nor Gentile, neither slave nor free, nor is there male and female, for you are all one in Christ Jesus. (Gal 3:26-28)

The group radiated this truth, and I absolutely *loved* it.

I attended the ASIF meetings almost every week that I was in London. Sometimes it took me two hours by public transport to get there. Sometimes, depending on where I was staying at the time and what I did after the meeting, my trip home took even longer. But even if it meant a long walk through the middle of the night in the rain, I didn't mind.

One evening when we were sharing prayer concerns, one of the girls mentioned that she was returning home to Lebanon, which at the time was in a state of civil war. In a few weeks she was going to be in a war zone! I compared this with the sorts of prayer requests I was used to hearing back in Australia, like "Can you pray for my exam on Friday?" Of course it's good to pray for everything, and God certainly is interested in our exams, but this girl's prayer request was on a completely different level. My Christian faith grew through meeting and praying for Christians whose lives and struggles were often so different from my own.

One of the best friends I made in the group was Veloo, a Tamil Malaysian man in his mid-thirties. We became close through spending a lot of time together studying the Bible, praying and socializing. The ASIF crowd always had something planned. With the variety of nationalities in the group there was no real cultural norm, so nights out might include anything from a prayer meeting to a movie, a Christian sing-a-long, a show, a sharing of testimonies or a meal. Several times we ended up sleeping on Veloo's floor for the night.

A few months after I became part of the ASIF group, some of us decided to go to the Scottish Highlands during the week. Most of the group went up a day earlier than I did, but Peter (another Australian) and I caught the Monday evening overnight bus to Fort William. It was a 12-hour trip via Glasgow during which Peter and I talked for many hours. I also discovered that a girl on the bus was a Christian from the Isle of Skye, so I spoke with her for a few hours too. It was a great trip, but I emerged from the bus badly in want of sleep.

The group at Fort William included Christians from Australia, Germany, Japan, Denmark, Malaysia and Kenya. For four days we walked, talked, hiked, cycled, ate, prayed, and studied the Bible together. We scaled Ben Nevis (the tallest mountain on the British Isles), and visited the Isle of Skye and Loch Ness (home to the fabled monster). I also submerged myself in a particularly icy mountain stream with a mad Dane called Nicklas, proving that… actually, I'm not quite sure what we were proving!

One evening in the youth hostel where we were all staying, I was talking with Belinda, an Australian girl who had been at the welcome desk on my first night at All Souls. The more we spoke, the more familiar her story sounded—there was her hometown, the fact that she'd been an exchange student in Germany and was a Christian, her appearance… Then the penny dropped: Belinda's grandmother was my godmother. Her father was my second cousin. I'd met all of her family in Australia a few years before, but she'd been in Germany. We created something of a scene when the connection finally dawned on us, and we quickly became very firm friends.

In mid-July of that year, about 50 of us from ASIF went to Ashburnham Place (a country house in Kent) for a weekend. There were Bible talks, Bible studies, prayers, and various other activities including a movie about the great missionary to China, Hudson Taylor. I turned 21 that weekend, and on the Saturday night they held a surprise birthday celebration for me with a speech and a cake. I was genuinely moved.

The ASIF group really was a very positive Christian environment—Bible reading, prayer and testimonies infused most things we did, and we had a lot of fun together. Despite our different backgrounds there was a marked unity among us, and relationships between men and women were conducted in a way that honoured Christ. It was a great model of Christian fellowship for me.

Given the nature of the group, people were always coming and going. Farewells were frequent and often poignant. My own farewell was held just before I left in mid-September. As usual, we all crowded into Veloo's flat—three Malaysians, three Australians, a Canadian, a Finn, a Kenyan, a Ugandan, an American and a guy from Japan. We ate, talked, sang, prayed and gave short speeches. We said our goodbyes and, as I'd often done before, I slept on Veloo's floor for the night.

Some ASIF members (such as the Australians) returned to countries where you can easily find good strong evangelical churches. Others, however, returned to places where fellow Christians and evangelical churches are few and far between. It was very hard for these people to leave the group. Eva had seen hundreds come and go over the years, and knew she couldn't promise to pray for everyone who passed through the group. But she always said, "I will pray for you when I think of you". This struck me as wise. She also reminded people that being a Christian means you never really have to say goodbye. Eva is no longer with us, but I (and many others) can look forward to the day when the ASIF Christians and countless others from all nations will be gathered together with Eva and with our Saviour (Rev 21:3-4).

The All Souls' ASIF group has been one of the biggest influences on my Christian life. I sometimes wonder how my life in London, and since, would have been different if I hadn't sought out its fellowship. Some Christians may not seek out fellowship when they're overseas because they are shy, or because they've had bad Christian fellowship experiences in the past, or simply because they don't know where to go. This last obstacle can be overcome easily with a bit of research, either before leaving home or once you're overseas. (And if you're not travelling yourself but you know someone who's going overseas, why not point them in the direction of any good churches you know about, do a bit of research on their behalf, or encourage them to do some research themselves?)

Shyness and negative experiences are possibly harder to overcome and can certainly make seeking out fellowship more challenging. If you've experienced either, God knows how you feel. Jesus is not "unable to empathize with our weaknesses" (Heb 4:15). He knows you, understands you, and wants you to have fellowship with other believers—and he'll answer your prayers for comfort and strength.

Admittedly, it can be hard to break into a church. Almost ten years after my initial time at All Souls, I went back to visit while I was in London for a few weeks. Though none of my old friends were attending that night, I was really looking forward to being there. It was a good service but afterwards, try as I might, I couldn't seem to get into a good conversation with anyone. I tried various people and adopted various strategies like hanging around where the coffee and tea were being served, but all to no avail. After maybe half an hour of trying, feeling a little dejected, I started to leave.

Just as I was walking out the front door, I heard someone call my name. It was Louise, a girl with whom I'd attended church in Sydney many years before. I didn't even know she was living in London. I went back in, she introduced me to her friends, and we all went out for coffee. A group of them invited me to dinner during that week, and the following Sunday I was in church meeting people and introducing them to others.

You may not always be fortunate enough to bump into someone you know, but my experience illustrates the fact that often you simply need to get that initial break. I've found the best way to do this is to join something—for example, a newcomers' group, a fellowship group, or a Bible study group. (Again, if you are not travelling yourself but happen to be reading this anyway, why not be on the lookout for visitors and travellers who may turn up at your church, and make them welcome?)

Fellowship is important, as Hebrews 10 tells us:

> And let us consider how we may spur one another on toward love and good deeds, not giving up meeting together, as some are in the habit of doing, but encouraging one another—and all the more as you see the Day approaching. (Heb 10:24-25)

Visiting churches

Obviously you can't join a church when you're moving around, but there's still great value in making a one-off visit to a church as you're passing through on a Sunday. Even if you don't have an opportunity to talk to anyone, hearing God's word preached and explained is always beneficial. And you never know what opportunities God will give you to encourage others. Some churches give travellers an opportunity during the service to encourage the congregation. A few times in Africa, for example, I've been asked to say a few words and bring greetings from my church in Australia.

Visiting a church can also lead to mutual encouragement with other believers in less formal ways. On my last solo overseas backpacking trip, I spent ten days in Bali and Lombok—I had some frequent flyer points that I had to use or lose, and I didn't want to let them go to waste. I planned my itinerary so that I'd be in the capital, Denpasar, on the two Sundays I was away. A friend had been part of a church there when he'd been working in that area a few years earlier, so that's where I decided to visit.

On my first Sunday night in Bali I went to the service, held in a function room at a hotel, and enjoyed the fellowship in this congregation that was made up predominantly of expats. After the service I was invited out for dinner with a small group that included a Malaysian man called Chan. The following Sunday I had afternoon tea with Chan, went to church, and went out for dinner again afterwards with a group of church people. I really appreciated Chan's efforts. We should never underestimate the impact that a bit of hospitality shown to a stranger can have.

For the sake of honesty I should confess that there have been times abroad when I haven't gone to church. Sometimes there were good reasons, but other times I was simply slack or fearful. No doubt, I missed out.

Visiting missionaries

Visiting missionaries can also be a helpful form of fellowship —as long as you make sure ahead of time that your visit will be convenient and welcome.

A number of years ago, Katherine, a missionary associated with my church, was serving in an Eastern European country. One of my previous Bible study groups had supported her with prayer and letters, so when I realized that my travels would take me close to where she was living I asked whether she'd like a visit. She said that she would, so I spent a few days in the city where she worked. I explored the city, learned more about her ministry, and met some of her Christian and non-Christian friends. It was interesting meeting people I'd known up until then only as names on prayer letters. I still get Katherine's prayer letters, and I've now been praying for her for more than 25 years.

Connecting with other Christian organizations

Linking up with a Christian organization is another good way to find fellowship overseas. If you're involved with an organization of Christian surfers or lawyers or nurses in your home country, for example, why not contact the corresponding organization in the country you're visiting? Another option is to attend a Christian convention or course in another country.

A number of years ago I was fortunate enough to attend the Maramon Christian Convention in Kerala, India. I was there for work, but it proved to be a great way to meet Indian believers. The convention, organized by the Mar Thoma Syrian Church, is one of the largest Christian conferences in the world. The main meetings were held in the dry riverbed of the Pampa River under a temporary structure of bamboo and thatched banana leaves. On the final weekend, a crowd of around 100,000 packed under this structure to listen to the speakers.

I befriended an Indian lawyer, Vijay, who was involved in running the conference. He was extremely hospitable, welcoming me into his home and introducing me to his family. One afternoon I asked him how he met his wife. Vijay looked a little surprised. "Well, err, my parents lived in… and her parents lived in… and they knew each other from…" Of course, it eventually dawned on me—it was an arranged marriage.

Another gentleman I met at the convention was a senior figure with an interdenominational Christian organization in India. I mentioned to him that I was going to a certain city in central India to visit an English friend, and he encouraged me to visit the family of Mary, one of the workers in his organization in that city.

So, the following week, courtesy of a rickshaw and a motorbike, I arrived at Mary's house around midday. I met Mary and her parents and her brother, and was treated to a lavish Indian meal. Afterwards we looked at family photos and Christian magazines, discussed ministry, watched some cricket, and prayed together. I learned that Mary's brother was struggling with his faith. Being a Christian in his workplace in this Hindu-Muslim dominated area brought decided challenges and disadvantages, and I was pleased to learn afterwards that my visit had been an encouragement to him.

Visiting Christian relatives and friends

If you are fortunate enough to have Christian relatives living overseas, this gives you another opportunity for fellowship. Relatives usually like meeting other relatives, and this is particularly the case when both parties, even if they're distant relations, are believers. Barriers of age, gender and culture simply evaporated, for example, when I visited my distant cousin Olive, the cool 80-year-old who drove me through the Cotswolds and to Stratford-upon-Avon in a zippy little car.

Catching up with Christian friends overseas is a no-brainer if you're visiting their part of the world, but give some thought ahead of time to how you can make the most of your visit. What can you discuss with them, give to them, or pray about with them? I'm all for talking football, shopping and travel plans, but make sure you discuss things of greater substance, too. As it says in Proverbs 27:17, "As iron sharpens iron, so one person sharpens another". Don't waste the opportunity with those who live far away to sharpen and encourage each other.

One good ASIF friend I made during my time in London was a Finnish girl by the name of Heidi. Some years later I had the opportunity to drop in on her in her native Finland. Heidi had found it difficult to connect with a good church when she returned home, and by the time I visited she had a non-Christian boyfriend named Tommi. Tommi was a great guy but not a believer.

One evening a few days into my stay, Heidi and I chatted for a few hours about Christianity and about ASIF while the Eurovision Song Contest played on television in the background (it's funny the things you remember). She showed me a couple of scrapbooks she'd kept from her time at church in London, with photographs and messages that clearly meant a lot to her. The fellowship she'd had in the ASIF group obviously still had an impact on her, all these years later. We had a really great time reminiscing about the old days. I think it's fair to say that the Finnish music industry had a less positive evening—their entrant finished in last place.

The next day threw up something of an ethical quandary for me. Heidi and Tommi took me to his family's summer-house—a cottage on an island in a lake surrounded by forest. You can't get more Finnish than that! We travelled out to the island in a small boat and spent a few idyllic hours shooting air rifles at tin cans, playing badminton and drinking coffee... but awkwardness loomed. The thing was, Tommi was dead-set on the idea that we all enjoy a particular Finnish speciality together: a sauna.

Tommi was clearly going out of his way to be as hospitable as possible to his girlfriend's religious friend from Australia, and generally I'm all for new cultural experiences. But there are limits, and I was doing my best to be a good ambassador for both Christ and country. I knew that Finns took saunas together unencumbered by any form of clothing, and while I was prepared to get naked with Tommi I really didn't think it would do me any good to do so with Heidi. Finns may be used to this sort of thing, but I certainly was not!

The dilemma occupied my mind all day. I aimed the air rifle (what should I do about the sauna?). I hit the shuttlecock (there's still the issue of that sauna). I took a sip of coffee (howamIgoingtogetoutofthesaunahelp!). And Tommi was not going to be put off. "So, how about we have sauna?" he suggested enthusiastically.

To my eternal gratitude, Heidi came to the rescue. "Ah, Tommi", she said, "I'm not feeling too good. You have sauna with Stephen. I think I'll lie down."

"But Heidi," Tommi protested, "he's visiting from Australia".

"No, Tommi, you two have sauna. I'll have a lie down."

I prayed a silent prayer of gratitude. It seemed that Heidi's spiritual-cultural radar was still functioning.

That changed everything. Tommi and I set off on a short brisk walk through the woods to the sauna, which was located near a jetty by the lake. We entered, stripped down and turned up the heat. Then, in good Finnish tradition, we hit ourselves with sticks and cooked sausages over the open coals before jumping into the lake. It was quite invigorating. Those Finns!

I kept in touch with Heidi for a few years, lost contact for a while, and recently touched base with her again. She's back on track with God and is working as a missionary in Africa—so this story has a happy ending.

A few years after my visit to Heidi, and nine years after my first trip overseas, I was back in Europe—in large part to attend Veloo's wedding. He was marrying a German Christian named Iris in her home town of Staufen. Invitations had been sent far and wide, and a number of other ASIF friends were going to be there as well. There was great excitement upon our arrival as we reunited with Veloo and met his fiancée and various family members and friends.

Staufen is a picturesque village on the edge of the Black Forest in the south-western corner of Germany. It has its own castle perched atop a hill at the edge of town. According to the famous German legend, it was here in Staufen that Faust sold his soul to the devil. In the days that followed our arrival, we hoped to put the location to a more constructive use.

Marriages in Germany must be performed at a registry office, and any church ceremony is held some time after the registry proceedings. Veloo and Iris's registry ceremony was held in the town hall on the afternoon I arrived. Afterwards we had afternoon tea back at Iris's place, and then walked up to a small chapel in the mountains where we held our own church service. We sang in English and German, and it felt very much like the old ASIF days.

The church wedding was still to come so we spent the next day getting things ready for the wedding as well as meeting friends and looking around the town. On the morning of the big day I found out that Veloo and Iris wanted some of us to perform a skit at their wedding reception that very night. "Do they really want a skit at their wedding reception?" I quietly wondered. Oh, well, when in Rome…

The church wedding, conducted in both German and English in the Staufen Protestant Church, was followed by a bizarre (at least to me) ritual where Veloo and Iris ran underneath a parachute as it was raised and lowered. It was lots of fun, and really added to the occasion. But it was at the dinner and reception that the celebrations really kicked into gear. Actually it was more variety show than reception—every person there (and there were a lot of people there!) seemed to be involved in some kind of performance. At one point I found myself involved in a short impromptu play that required me to get up on stage and impersonate a rooster. If you're going to make a fool of yourself then you may as well do it properly, so I threw myself into the role.

Eventually it was time for the ASIF crowd's skit, which we presented in English, German, and a little-known ancient Urdu dialect, and which portrayed the variety and randomness of life in the ASIF group. The plot involved a large and varied cast of characters turning up at Veloo's flat in London—including an ASIF member's sister's ex-boyfriend's tax consultant as well as a passing jogger—and ended with everyone spending the night on his floor. After the skit, a couple of us spoke about the impact Veloo had had on our lives. I think that by the end, Veloo's new family and friends in Staufen understood the high regard in which many of us from around the globe hold Veloo. He's a fine Christian man through whom God has done so much for so many. It was such a thrill to be at his wedding.

Connecting with other travellers

I have sometimes travelled for long periods without meeting other believers. At other times it has seemed as if the vaults of heaven have opened and it's raining the regenerate—as was the case over a four-day period in Zimbabwe and Botswana.

On the first day I caught the bus from Masvingo to Bulawayo. It took about four hours and dropped me in the city centre in the early afternoon. I was sitting in a park eating lunch when an 18-year-old Zimbabwean spotted my striped polo shirt, which he mistook for a rugby shirt, and struck up a conversation. His name was Nyasha and he'd recently toured Australia with his school cricket team, so clearly we had a lot to discuss. We walked to a nearby hotel for a soft drink and chatted for a couple of hours. It turned out that he was a Christian, so we had even more to talk about. Later that day I was back at the youth hostel in Bulawayo, where I'd met Claudia a week earlier—the German medical student who had become a Christian. She was still there, so that evening we took up where we'd left off.

On the second day I caught the train to Francistown in Botswana—the one that stopped in the wilderness for seven hours—and that was the night I met the English girl, Kate, who had recently recommitted her life to Christ.

On the third day I travelled by bus across the top of the Kalahari to Maun, arriving after dark. Not wanting to pay for an expensive night in a hotel, I made my way to the local police station. The police gave me permission to pitch my tent behind their building (after questioning me to establish that I was not a South African spy!).

I awoke on the fourth day to discover that the back of the police station was, in fact, the middle of another road. Curious people and cows ambled by, discreetly peering at the novelty that had materialized overnight in the middle of their street. I quickly packed up and caught a lift to the edge of the Okavango Delta, where I checked into a lodge and pitched my tent in a more orthodox location. One of the tents near me belonged to David, a South African lawyer and—you guessed it—a Christian. His friend was not, and David was doing his best to be a good Christian witness to his mate. David told me later that my turning up and having dinner with them was both heartening for him and a helpful witness to his friend.

Sometimes there are ways we can make these encounters with other Christians more likely. My friends from church who drove around Europe in a van in the 70s did so with Australian flags and a Christian fish sticker clearly displayed on their vehicle. One morning while they were having breakfast in a camping area in Paris, there was a knock on the door. A curly-haired man was standing outside smiling. "Hi! You're Australians. You're Christians. So are we!" My friends invited this man and his wife to have a cup of tea and now, 40 years later, they're still very close friends.

What about dating?

What if you're not married, and while travelling you meet a lovely Christian person of the opposite sex to whom you're attracted? Should you consider dating? My advice is to be cautious. Because being overseas is inherently romantic and can also foster loneliness, it's possible to feel drawn to someone for whom we wouldn't have such feelings if we met them in the midst of normal life back home.

My personal view is that there's no reason to date someone unless there's at least the possibility that you might want to marry them at some point. In theory, there's no reason not to date and marry a person you meet overseas. But if that person normally lives in a different country from your own, you'll need to do some serious thinking about the potential future of the relationship. Where would you live, for example, and how would that impact other relationships and responsibilities? If you're thinking about dating someone you've met overseas, it would be helpful to talk through the situation with some Christians you trust.

While I was overseas I met an Australian girl I really liked. We spent time together but didn't enter into a relationship. Once we were both back in Australia the following year, we did date for a while. I think that for us, this was the wiser course.

There are lots of books that discuss dating from a Christian perspective, but if you do feel that it's godly, wise and appropriate to date another Christian you meet while travelling or living abroad, one of the most helpful things you can do is to set clear physical boundaries. Remember—you're dating, not married, so you don't have sex. In fact, you don't go anywhere near it. Sexual immorality entails any activity that deliberately arouses sexual desire for anyone other than your spouse. If you're dating, keep things in the area of affection, not arousal.

Ongoing relationships

When you're overseas, you often meet new people and travel with them for a few days before parting ways and never seeing each other again. It would be a full-time job to keep in contact with everyone you ever met, but saying goodbye to someone at a bus station or airport does not have to mean the end of your connection with each other. As Eva from ASIF used to say, "I will pray for you when I think of you". We can always pray for the people we've met on our travels. We may have no idea where they are today or how they're going, but God does. He takes our prayers and uses them for his purposes. I've lost contact with Nyasha, Claudia and David, but I can still pray for them.

I am still in contact, however, with a number of Christians I've met overseas—Veloo, Kate and Heidi, for example. Many of the people I've met mean a lot to me, and although we all live busy lives, a Christmas card, an email, or a Facebook post is always possible. It's great to hear about believers pushing on in their faith, and as the years go by I'm encouraged to hear about how their children are, too. A recent Christmas letter from a Canadian ASIF friend and his wife tells me that their son, now in his twenties, plays guitar on the music team in church. If only that sort of encouraging report was true for all my Christian friends!

As you might expect (and as we've seen above), people's

spiritual walks vary and life takes its toll on some. I think of one friend I met while travelling who has struggled with her Christian faith, has been abandoned by her husband, and is now doing her best as a single parent. I can think of another who, last time I heard, appeared to have been moving away from church life. Many Christian people I have met overseas struggle in the same ways that Christian friends do at home. When I think of these and others I know who are struggling, I pray for them and trust God to continue to work in their lives and hearts. Fortunately, amid all the spiritual attrition, there are plenty of good stories.

Ongoing country support

When people are listing the ongoing relationships they have from their overseas travels, they usually list people rather than places. But you can have enduring and ongoing associations with cities and countries you've visited as well as with individuals.

When you spend a reasonable period of time in one place you meet the locals, you learn how things operate, and you get a sense of the place. Part of the connection you develop as a Christian is an awareness of its spiritual and physical needs. At least, that is how it was for me after my first trip to Africa.

"What could I do for Africa?" I wondered after returning home. Africa had gotten not only under my skin but into my heart and inside my brain as well. I lived thousands of kilometres away in Australia, but it struck me that there were two things I could easily do: pray and give money. None of my church's missionaries were serving in Africa, so I decided to support a Christian organization that served God there. But which one?

I thought of the South African family I'd met on the Kariba Ferry who were involved with African Enterprise, a Christian organization that promotes ministry *to* Africans *by* Africans. I did some research and found out that its primary work is evangelism, but that it's also involved with discipleship, aid work and reconciliation ministry. This balance struck me as a good one, so I decided to join their mailing list, pray for their ministry, and support them financially.

More than a decade later, I'd completed some theological studies at Moore Theological College in Sydney. One day it occurred to me that I could make some short-term visits overseas to lecture in theology if anyone wanted me. If it was okay with Moore College, I could use teaching materials from its Department of External Studies (now called Moore Distance). The college was happy for me to do this, so I raised this idea with leaders at African Enterprise. They were keen on the idea and suggested that we trial it in Kenya and Uganda. So, a few months later, I taught a two-week biblical theology course in Nairobi and then another two-week course in Kampala.

The venture was such a success that, over the next few years, an ongoing ministry partnership between Moore College and African Enterprise developed. Its aim was to provide high-quality, low-cost, short-term theological education to untrained Christian leaders in Africa (of whom there are many). The idea was to put as many leaders as we could through six two-week courses over a one- to three-year period. We weren't there to tell them how to run their churches—they know their cultures better than we ever could—but to help them better understand the word of God. Since that first trial course, more than 35 part-time lecturers have taught around 1,200 students in eight African countries. Many students have completed six subjects, some 12, and a few 18. But the benefits go both ways. I've visited eight times now, and my fellow lecturers and I have always learned a great deal from the Africans with whom we've interacted. I've been truly blessed to be part of this program and I thank God for the thread of his work that, unbeknownst to me, began all those years ago on a ferry trip one sunny morning in Zimbabwe.

Unfortunately, not all countries in the world are as welcoming to the Christian faith as those in Sub-Saharan Africa. After my first working visit to India, I came home via Vietnam where I holidayed for two weeks with a friend. Near the end of that trip I travelled up to a town called Sapa, in an area where the Hmong ethnic minority group lives. When I returned home, I decided to do something to support the church there. I discovered that Vietnam did not treat Christians very well at all—in fact, the Christian organization Open Doors had ranked Vietnam as the ninth worst country in the world for persecuting Christians that year. But I also learned that there had been something of a Christian revival in the country, particularly amongst the Hmong people—apparently God had significantly used Christian radio broadcasts to reach people there. I discovered two Christian organizations that work in Vietnam: The Voice of the Martyrs and the Far East Broadcasting Company (FEBC). Since then, in my own small way, I've supported both of these ministries financially and with prayer.

These days I pray on different days for a different country or part of the world, including Sub-Saharan Africa, England,

Germany, Scandinavia, the Czech Republic and another Eastern European country. When I have friends who live or serve in Christian ministry in those places, my prayers can be more specific. But where my prayers are more general I know that "the Spirit helps us in our weakness" and that "the Spirit himself intercedes for us through wordless groans" (Rom 8:26).

Passing it on

Robbie, a friend who recently finished university, decided to backpack for six weeks in South-East Asia before starting full-time work. Before he left, I encouraged him to pray that while he was away God would lead him to Christians he could encourage and non-Christians he could point towards Christ. He took up the challenge, and God answered his prayers.

While staying at a lodge in Thailand he had a discussion about his faith one night with two guys who weren't believers. Others at the lodge were listening in, and the next day a man from Norway told Robbie how encouraged he'd been by what he'd overheard. This Norwegian, a Christian, attends a Lutheran church but is the only believer in his family. Hearing Robbie contend for the faith had really lifted his spirits.

Robbie really enjoyed spending time with this man, but more significant still was the mutual encouragement that had taken place—one of God's answers to his prayers.

Checklist for connecting with Christians

- Resolve to travel with God—spend time with him regularly.
- Track down Christian fellowship. If you're staying in one place for an extended period of time, join a church and get involved. Some prior research may help.
- If you're just passing through on a Sunday, find a service to attend. Again, prior research may help.
- Consider visiting other Christians—relatives, friends, missionaries and even organizations—with whom you have some connection.
- Consider attending Christian courses or conventions.
- Ask God to lead you to believers you can encourage, and be on the lookout for opportunities.
- Think about how you can support the Christians you meet, as well as Christian ministries in the countries you visit, on an ongoing basis.
- Expect that you will be tempted to do *none* of the things suggested in this checklist. Don't let sin ruin your time abroad—or your life.

4

CONNECTING WITH NON-CHRISTIANS

"You are the light of the world. A town built on a hill cannot be hidden. Neither do people light a lamp and put it under a bowl. Instead they put it on its stand, and it gives light to everyone in the house. In the same way, let your light shine before others, that they may see your good deeds and glorify your Father in heaven." (Matt 5:14-16)

It was over. The Maramon Christian Convention in Kerala had finished, and my work there was done. Being overseas, I'd decided to take one of my short add-on holidays before returning home. So, one warm February morning, I farewelled my hosts and caught a taxi to the town of Alappuzha. There I pulled out my *Lonely Planet* guide, put my pack on my back, and boarded a boat travelling south through the Keralan backwaters. I had returned to the circuit—this time in India.

On board I quickly spotted and fell into conversation with

two other fellow travellers—Maggie from Wales and Hanna from Belgium. We chatted happily as we enjoyed the beautiful eight-hour trip, sailing through narrow channels and wide expanses of water, past fields, houses and fishing boats. Children chased the boat along the banks as their parents busied themselves with their riverside chores. Every now and then we pulled into a village to drop off and pick up passengers.

At one of these stops another Westerner, also from Wales, joined us. He looked to be in his thirties, wore a bandana, and spoke in a slow, profound way. He'd been on the road for much longer than any of us had, and we soon discovered that his concerns had moved beyond simply meeting people and seeing new places. He had, we learned, been staying at an ashram. "It's run by India's only female guru", he told us. The man was fervent in his testimony about what this woman had done for him: "Man, I'm telling you, she changed my life". He gave the impression that he'd finally found whatever it was that he'd been looking for. We listened politely, and eventually he got off the boat at another village.

I felt sad for him, but decided to be circumspect in my comments. After all, I was no longer at a Christian convention; I was on the road, hanging out with open-minded, uber-tolerant travellers—or so I assumed. He was not long gone when Maggie, who wasn't burdened by any such circumspection, voiced her opinion: "What a jerk!"

That dismissive remark didn't in any way sum up Maggie's overall life philosophy—she was a very friendly and non-dismissive sort of person—but the stark contrast between the two Welsh people highlighted for me the simple truth that at any point in time some people are spiritually searching while others are not.

Maggie, Hanna and I travelled on and arrived later that evening in Varkala, a picturesque village situated along the top of a red-earth cliff that drops about 15 metres to an idyllic white-sand beach. We decided to dig in for a few days of serious rest.

Our group quickly grew as we linked up with like-minded backpackers. There was Josh, an American who was travelling around by motorcycle. Mark and Amy were both from England. Mark seemed like he had probably attended a posh English public school and Amy was the girlfriend of a moderately famous English rock musician. Garry and Anna, a couple, were also from England. They seemed a little rougher than the rest of us. Garry had tattoos down one arm and had played guitar with a hard-core metal band. He told me that in earlier days he'd been a punk with an orange Mohawk. It was a great group, and we spent a very enjoyable few days together.

One morning I was sitting by myself in one of the pagodas reading my Bible when one of the group joined me. We ended up having a good long talk about life in general, about our lives, and in particular about Christianity. This person was quite interested and open. Of my new cluster of friends, which one do you think would have been up for this sort of interaction? It was Garry, the ex-punk. He told me he'd lived a rough life for about 12 years but was now getting himself together. I'm not sure what sort of long-term impact our discussion had, but I pray it was a link in a chain that might one day lead him to Christ.

Visually, Varkala was stunning; life at the beach resembled a tropical paradise. But away from the tourist strip, it was no economic paradise. Locals survived by fishing and farming, living at just above subsistence level. Walking north up the coast one morning, I watched fishermen pulling in their nets. I helped one group for a while—it was hard, labour-intensive work—before retiring to sit under a tree. No doubt many looked to supplement their income. I was not long settled when my idle thoughts were interrupted by a local guy offering to sell me some grass products (by which I don't mean woven baskets).

More significantly, the area was no spiritual paradise. While Kerala may be one of the more Christian areas of India, more than half its population is Hindu and more than a quarter is Muslim. Amongst the travellers there was probably even less of a Christian presence. I was wandering around one evening looking for Josh when I stumbled upon a fairly relaxed group of about 30 Westerners sitting around smoking while a couple of them quietly played a flute and some drums. There was a fair bit of hippie culture about the place. While the friends with whom I had linked up were somewhat less 'alternative', we too sat around late one night chatting until the small hours, with a few in our little crowd smoking grass and downing alcohol. (Traveller alert: I didn't smoke any weed or go over my two-drink limit but had I been so inclined, or weaker willed, I could have easily done so. What would you have done?)

Mission field or minefield?

As I said earlier, it is generally the people we meet on our travels who make our time overseas so enriching and stimulating. But the fact that these encounters often take place in very pleasant surroundings shouldn't blind us to the fact that, when we're abroad, we're in a hard-core mission field *and* minefield. The backpacking circuit, for example, is no church camp. There are great opportunities for the Christian, but there are also great dangers. Similarly, living overseas is no Sunday School picnic—it brings you strongly under the influence of those with whom you spend your time. It's not just a question of how you'll impact them, but also of how they'll impact you.

First, let's think about the mission field. In the previous chapter we discussed the kinds of opportunities we have to encourage other believers in their faith. But given that the majority of people in the world are not followers of Jesus, it's likely that most of the people we meet on our travels won't be believers. If we're walking closely with God, the needs about us will be obvious. God's Spirit will help us to view the crowds in the same way that Jesus did:

> When he saw the crowds, he had compassion on them, because they were harassed and helpless, like sheep without a shepherd. Then he said to his disciples, "The harvest is plentiful but the workers are few. Ask the Lord of the harvest, therefore, to send out workers into his harvest field." (Matt 9:36-38)

This is a good prayer to pray—and we can be part of the answer to it.

It can actually be easier to have spiritual discussions with people when we're overseas than when we are at home. Travellers are often more relaxed and open, being away from the stresses and strains of everyday life. The experience of a church friend who recently returned from the United States reflects my own: "When you meet people travelling, you talk about your life—where you come from, what you do, your hobbies and your beliefs. I was proud to say that I was a Christian. In some ways people are more open to talking, knowing that after a day or so they may never see you again. Back here in Australia, in normal life, it's harder. Overseas everyone talks about what they believe."

But life away from home is also a minefield. In a discussion about the drinking culture often found within the backpacking community, a friend once told me, "People go out a lot at night and drink heavily at bars. In this sort of environment it would be easy to go overboard." Paul's warning to the Christians in Ephesus is relevant to us here:

> Be very careful, then, how you live—not as unwise but as wise, making the most of every opportunity, because the days are evil. (Eph 5:15-16)

The days *are* evil. We need to think and act very carefully and wisely. The lifestyles of the people we meet, and the cultures to which we're exposed overseas, will often be very different from those in our Christian communities. You might well *survive* abroad, but will your relationship with God *grow* and *deepen* while you're away? At an even more basic level, will you be able to resist the temptations of sexual immorality, drugs and alcohol abuse? How will you deal with the non-Christian world views and lifestyles you encounter?

After reading chapter 7 of this book, praying through the issues, and speaking with wise Christians about your plans, you may actually decide *not* to go abroad (or at least, not yet). Or you might decide that you should travel with another Christian or as part of a Christian group. Mission fields are there for the reaping, but minefields can kill.

As Christians, we can be thermostats or thermometers. Thermostats regulate the temperature of their surroundings, while thermometers simply reflect the temperature of their surroundings. We want to be travelling thermostats. To do this, we need to work hard at the sorts of things discussed in chapter 1—maintaining our relationship with God, being disciplined about our devotions, seeking out Christian fellowship, and asking for prayer support from Christian family and friends. We also need to implement the sort of thinking that we'll discuss in chapters 6 and 7. Doing these things will mean that you'll be better equipped to "let your light shine before others, that they may see your good deeds and glorify your Father in heaven" (Matt 5:16).

The mission field

Right before his ascension, Jesus told his disciples:

> "But you will receive power when the Holy Spirit comes on you; and you will be my witnesses in Jerusalem, and in all Judea and Samaria, and to the ends of the earth." (Acts 1:8)

Over the centuries there have been many Christians who have gone into full-time cross-cultural mission work, often at incredible cost and with much self-sacrifice, in an effort to take the message of Jesus to the ends of the earth. While our backpacking holidays, study exchanges, working vacations, gap years and temporary sojourns in foreign parts are hardly comparable to the sacrifices some have made, we do have opportunities when we travel to contribute to God's work in the world in our own humble ways. I've always liked the maxim that evangelism is simply one beggar telling another beggar where to find bread.

Part of this is praying regularly, as I've said—asking God to lead us to other believers we can encourage and to non-believers with whom we can be some sort of Christian witness. If we pray this way, our experience will no doubt reflect that of Paul in Athens almost 2000 years ago: "When they [the Athenians] heard about the resurrection of the dead, some of them sneered, but others said, 'We want to hear you again on this subject'" (Acts 17:32). And some of them did end up believing (v. 34). We can expect that when we pray for opportunities and take them, we'll receive a similar range of responses.

I am far from being the world's greatest evangelist. I've often been slack and forgetful, and I've squandered opportunities. But as you'll see in the stories that follow, I've often prayerfully done my best, too. And what I've found is that there are people interested in the gospel everywhere—often in the most unlikely places.

Many are interested

One of the highlights of my first trip overseas was a five-day tour of the Cotswolds with my cricket club. The Cotswolds is an impossibly picturesque section of southern England, with rolling hills, country lanes, villages with thatched-roofed houses and historic churches. Around each corner lurks a scene that could easily find its way onto a postcard. And of course each village had a cricket team.

We stayed in the small market town of Chipping Camden

at a hotel that had once been a 16th-century coaching inn. As the week progressed, a routine developed: sleep in, eat a late breakfast, lie around, play an afternoon cricket game, socialize in the clubhouse afterwards, return to the hotel for a late dinner, then socialize some more in the hotel bar until about midnight. I got to know a number of my teammates much better during that week. As usual, I limited my intake of alcohol.

On the last night of the tour we followed the usual routine except that we stayed up much later, into the small hours of the morning. Sometime after three o'clock I realized that Clare—a young woman with whom we'd been talking—needed to return to her accommodation. Since it was so late, I offered to walk her home.

As soon as we were outside, she turned to me and asked, "Does it bother you that the other guys hassle you about being a Christian?"

I must admit that I hadn't felt particularly harassed. Most of the banter about my beliefs was good-natured, and in response I tended to give as good as I got. "Not really", I said. "It's all pretty lighthearted. In fact, if anything, I feel sorry for them."

This took her by surprise. "What do you mean?"

So there in the darkness of the early morning, we sat on the kerbside and I told her about following Jesus. I may even have given her a gospel tract, but I can't quite remember. Clare seemed genuinely interested in what I had had to say. I frequently think of that cricket tour, and particularly of that last night. And often when I think of Clare, I pray for her.

We can find people who are interested in the gospel in the most unexpected situations. A few weeks earlier I had been out in central London with some friends from ASIF. To cut a long story short, various circumstances resulted in Belinda (my second cousin once removed) and me finding ourselves stranded in the East End in the early morning. With limited options we decided to sit on the sidewalk and talk for a few hours until the trains started to run again. At about 5am, a man jogged past and looked at us. He jogged further down the road, stopped, and then turned and made his way back to us.

"Are you guys okay?" He seemed like a bit of a rough diamond, but he was a jogger—usually an indicator of some sort of reliability—and he was friendly. We explained what had happened. He thought for a bit. "Do you guys want to come back to my place for a cup of tea?"

Looking back I wonder how smart we were to accept his invitation, but we did, and the three of us walked for a few minutes down the road to his flat. As we walked, he told us that he felt as if someone had told him to go back and invite us to tea. Belinda and I began to talk about church and Christianity, and he seemed interested.

"You know", he confessed as we sat at his kitchen table a short while later, "recently I've been drawing a lot of devils".

At this point, I suspect both Belinda and I upped the intensity of our silent prayers! Our host pulled out some sheets of paper and showed us some of his drawings. They did indeed look like they could have been representations of devils—not that we really knew. We were now on a heightened level of alert.

In the end, our East End jogging mate was nothing other than hospitable and friendly. He seemed to think that our meeting had been ordained in some way—which, no doubt, it had. We invited him along to church. I don't think he ended up at a Sunday service, but he did come to an ASIF event. He was clearly a nice but troubled person who was searching. Again, I hope that we were a link in a chain to his finding Christ.

I've been involved in many evangelistic discussions with interested travellers and locals over the years. I'd encourage you to be bold, and to look for and take opportunities when they arise. You never know whose heart will be open. It's exciting when God uses our prayers and willingness to speak as part of his transnational purposes. I should say, however, that mixed in with many positive encounters are others that have appeared to go nowhere.

Many are not interested

My comment rose into the air like aerial sewage and hovered in the tropical heat. Their expressions changed slowly from reluctant comprehension to controlled dismay. After hours of unceasing conversation, the silence gaped like an open wound.

The three of us—Thomas, Christiane and I—were sitting with our backpacks on the ferry from Lombok to Bali. My two new friends were from Switzerland, both social workers. When they'd eventually got around to asking what I did, I had tried to soften the blow by explaining that I used to be a lawyer and then I worked in the media before I began my current course of study.

Thomas and Christiane stared awkwardly out to sea. "Errr... I'm studying at theological college", I repeated, trying to sound as if I was discussing something as ordinary as the weather.

They were two of the nicest people I'd ever met—articulate, informed, friendly and unpretentious—but this information had absolutely floored them. This was clearly going to be nothing like my conversation a few days earlier with a Swedish girl I met, who had expressed interest in a gospel website I told her about as we travelled by bus around central Bali.

Perhaps some clarification was necessary: "Um… Bible college. You know, about God… Jesus… Christianity…"

Boy, that horizon had them completely transfixed. They were from Geneva, so I tried a different angle: "Hey, Calvin was from Geneva", I ventured. The comment got about as much traction as a request for tofu at a steakhouse.

If I had said, "Oh! Did you think I said 'theological college'? No, no. What I actually said was that I club baby seals to death for a living", I think they would have laughed with sheer relief. "Oh, thank goodness! We thought you said you were studying at theological college!"

Eventually I let them off the hook by moving to a different topic, and the conversation returned to normal. We enjoyed the rest of the day together, even eating breakfast together the following morning before our paths took us in different directions. Whatever associations they may have had with Christianity or theological college, we parted on very good terms—and I trust God used the encounter for his purposes.

But sometimes people can be more than just a little awkward or disinterested when they discover our beliefs. A few years after the fall of the Iron Curtain, I was travelling through Eastern Europe. At the time there were a few backpackers and other travellers, but the tourist hoards had not yet really begun to descend on these parts.

Early one Saturday morning I arrived at a bus station in Budapest, Hungary, to catch a bus to Zakopane at the foot of the Tatra Mountains in southern Poland. I'd just spent three very full and interesting days poking around the Hungarian capital and surrounding countryside, but I'd been on my own so I was keen to meet up with some fellow travellers. To my great delight I found myself sitting near Max and Maddie from Wisconsin in the United States. They were the sort of adventurous people you often meet in vaguely out of the way places. We seemed to hit it off well as we talked and exchanged stories during the trip.

When we arrived in Zakopane, the three of us booked into the youth hostel and had dinner together. It was a nice relief to have some companionship, and I assumed we'd probably hang out for a couple of days together before heading off in different directions.

When we met for breakfast the following morning, I was preparing to suggest a few ideas for the day when, to my surprise, an uncomfortable looking Max said, "Ah, well, Stephen, there have been a few changes".

It was a strange turn of phrase. He continued awkwardly, "I think Maddie and I might go it alone today".

Right! I maintained a composed expression. "Sure, no problems", I said, trying to sound unconcerned. What on earth had gone on here?

Max then apologized to me for any bad language he had used the previous day. Like most Westerners, Max used the occasional profanity, but it was hardly close to anything I might have considered offensive. I don't generally expect non-Christians to speak without using a smattering of swearwords.

And then it clicked—they'd probably seen me reading my Bible the previous afternoon. My guess was that Max had no problem with this, but it seemed like it had freaked out his girlfriend for some reason. Max looked embarrassed, whereas Maddie looked tense. It was one of the few times on my travels when temporary companions were not only disinterested in my beliefs but wanted to shut down our relationship because of them (at least, I think that was why).

So we parted company. I spent two days walking through this lovely area… by myself. One day I hiked up a white-peaked mountain and built a small snowman—probably the best friend I made in that beautiful place. But as far as persecution goes, I guess it was pretty light.

We shouldn't be discouraged when negative responses come our way—after all, the same thing happened to Jesus, and he taught that this very thing would take place. We shouldn't be deflated when negative responses come our way—ultimately, our significance is in Christ and not in the passing attitudes of others. And we shouldn't be dissuaded when negative responses come our way—we need to keep putting God first in our life, and you never know how he might use the encounter for his good purposes. And for those times when all this is easier said than done and the negative response cuts deeply, remember that we can pray to a God who is able to "empathize with our weaknesses" (Heb 4:15) and who is "close to the brokenhearted" (Ps 34:18).

Cross-cultural mission

Most of the locals I've met when I've been travelling in non-Western countries have not been Christians. I've gotten to know some fairly well, and on certain occasions have had the opportunity to mention something about my faith; but between cultural differences and (sometimes) language barriers it can be hard to know what actually gets through.

Vietnam has been one of my favourite travel destinations. When I travelled to Sapa in the north-western part of the country, I was surprised to be greeted in fluent English by a young girl around the age of ten from the Hmong ethnic group. She'd apparently learned English by speaking with tourists, and was selling bracelets and clothing, some of which I eventually bought. Whenever we saw each other over the next few days, she would usually stop for a chat. She was from a village about seven kilometres away, but spent most of the week in Sapa selling goods.

We got on well, and I wondered if there was anything I could say to her about Christianity that was appropriate and that would make sense to her. I knew she couldn't read, so the best I came up with was to show her a few photographs. "This is a picture of Sydney, which is where I come from. This is my family. And these are a few of my friends from church. Do you know about church?"

She nodded.

"Well, I'm a Christian and I go to church." It wasn't much, but it was the best I could do. If I made a good impression on her then at least she'd have a positive association with Christianity. On the day I left, she turned up at 6.30am to wave me off as the minibus pulled out. While cross-cultural witness can be a challenge, God is still able to use our humble efforts.

As I mentioned in the previous chapter, I later discovered there had been something of a Christian revival amongst the Hmong, so there probably were followers of Jesus amongst her tribal grouping. But because of the persecution of believers in Vietnam, life would get tough for her if she ever became a Christian.

Know *what* you believe

It is crucial for Christians, whether overseas or not, to know what we believe and why we believe it. Knowing *what* we believe—in particular the gospel, and in a way we can easily explain—is clearly important, so that we can share it with others when the opportunity arises. We also need to know *why* we believe the gospel so we can respond to the questions and objections people may raise about our faith.

Learning a gospel outline is one of the most useful things we can do, both for ourselves and for others. As Paul writes in Romans 1:16:

> I am not ashamed of the gospel, because it is the power of God that brings salvation to everyone who believes: first to the Jew, then to the Gentile.

For some reason, learning how to explain this message clearly and concisely is something many believers resist doing. Most Christians *recognize* the gospel when they hear it—"Yes, that's the gospel!" or "No, that's a false gospel!"—and assume this means that they can *reproduce* it in a clear and simple way when they need to. Sadly, this is often not the case.

I once gave a surprise anonymous survey to 100 people who were attending some seminars on evangelism that I was running. I gave them two minutes and asked them to write down a brief gospel outline on a scrap of paper. Looking through the responses later, I concluded that about half of these people could explain the gospel. But this meant that the other half could not (and remember, these were people who were sufficiently keen to come to a class on evangelism). I'm sure most of them would have *recognized* the gospel if they'd heard it; their problem was *reproducing* the message.

There are a number of good gospel summaries that Christians can learn: *Two Ways to Live*,[11] *The Four Spiritual Laws*, *The Bridge to Life*, and the 'God-person-God what-if-you-do what-if-you-don't' outline I learned as a young man. Being familiar with a summary like one of these can give us great confidence when we're explaining our faith.

But of course gospel conversations are just that—*conversations*, not *recitations*. We can't simply recite what we've learned, or dump all our points onto some poor unsuspecting target. We aim to communicate saving truths, as the situation allows, within the context of a genuine conversation with another person. We listen and respond to what the other person says. We share thoughts of our own as appropriate.

More often than not, we'll get to explain a part of the gospel or we'll have a chance to give our personal testimony, but opportunities to explain the entire gospel to an interested conversation partner can be rare. Having said that, if you ask someone whether they would like to hear a summary of the Christian message, they might very well say yes. Whether we get the opportunity to discuss all or only part of the gospel, however, the important thing is to participate in a positive spiritual conversation.

As even a brief exchange about spiritual beliefs usually reveals, most nonbelievers have rejected a Christian faith that

11 See the appendix.

they haven't understood. Most wrongly assume that someone becomes a Christian by being a good person, or by going to church, or by being born into a certain family or culture, or by identifying oneself as Christian on a census document, or by developing a predilection for stained-glassed windows. Tragic misunderstandings are commonplace.

Very few nonbelievers know that we're saved not by what we *do* but by receiving what Christ has *done*. We are saved not by our *works* but by God's *grace*. Many nonbelievers have a vague idea *that* God loves them, but very few have a clue as to *how much* God loves them, what he has self-sacrificially done for them on the cross, or from what he offers to rescue them. As I've found so often when abroad, opportunities will arise to explain these life-changing truths to a fellow traveller or an interested local—so it's worth being prepared for these moments.

You might even pack a few gospel outlines or booklets in your luggage.[12] You don't want to force your literature onto unwilling recipients, but there are times when you can naturally say to someone, "If you'd like to think further about what we've been discussing, here's a short booklet that you might find helpful".

Know *why* you believe it

My friend Robbie often found himself in gospel conversations with other backpackers in South-East Asia. Some were genuinely interested, while others were more antagonistic.

12 Another good option is to pack some copies of *The Essential Jesus* (Matthias Media, Sydney, 2008). This small booklet contains the Gospel of Luke along with some introductory material that very briefly summarizes the story of the Bible leading up to Luke's Gospel. It also includes a short explanation of the gospel.

Here are some of the questions he was frequently asked:

- What about all the suffering and injustice in the world?
- What's with this whole no-sex-before-marriage thing?
- What about homosexuality?
- Why should we believe the Bible?
- What about those who have never heard about Christianity?
- How do you know that Christianity is right? Isn't that just your opinion?

It is easy to see why Westerners travelling in the East might have these sorts of concerns. How well equipped to respond did Robbie feel? Could he explain not only *what* he believed, but also *why* he believed it?

"Sometimes I felt adequately prepared", he told me, "but at other times much less so".

As Robbie discovered, most travellers who are willing to talk about spiritual matters will ask questions. Some ask out of a genuine interest to know the answers, while others may simply raise what they consider to be unanswerable questions in an effort to keep the gospel at arm's length. Regardless of the reasons behind their queries, it's usually best to provide some sort of kind, respectful response.

But the possibility of having to do this can frighten the life out of some believers. What if I don't know what to say? What if they make me look like an idiot? And even, perhaps: What if they make me doubt my own beliefs?

Rest assured on this last point. As Christians, we have no need to fear the truth—Jesus is, after all, "the way and the truth and the life" (John 14:6). It's also a comfort to know that there probably aren't any questions about the faith that

Christians haven't already had to answer. As a result, there are some very good books and resources on what's known as 'Christian apologetics' that we can read, watch or listen to in preparation for these sorts of conversations. Some good examples include Tim Keller's *The Reason for God* and Paul Little's *Know Why You Believe*. I'd encourage everyone to take advantage of resources like these before going overseas.

But let's be realistic. Even if we prepare well, we may still be asked the occasional question that we can't answer. But this isn't a problem—no-one expects us to know everything. When this happens, there's nothing wrong with simply saying something like: "That's a very good question, and I haven't thought about it before. Why don't you give me your email address and I'll send you some thoughts once I've looked into it a bit?"

The sort of preparation I'm suggesting here will help us not only when we're travelling or living overseas, but also throughout our lives in general. Addressing these sorts of questions has not only given me confidence in speaking with others; it's also been a great encouragement for my own Christian faith.

Knowing *what* we believe and *why* we believe it is really just our obedient response to Peter's instruction in 1 Peter 3:15:

> But in your hearts revere Christ as Lord. Always be prepared to give an answer to everyone who asks you to give the reason for the hope that you have. But do this with gentleness and respect…

Live like you believe it

The gospel is the power of God for salvation, and people need to hear its message. When they hear it, they often have legitimate questions. But people who are considering whether or not they'll follow Jesus are also influenced by another powerful factor: what the believer is like. Do they practise what they preach? Are they a loving, engaging person? When travellers and locals meet them, what sort of ambassador for Christ are they meeting? Peter teaches on this point in 1 Peter 2:

> Dear friends, I urge you, as foreigners and exiles, to abstain from sinful desires, which wage war against your soul. Live such good lives among the pagans that, though they accuse you of doing wrong, they may see your good deeds and glorify God on the day he visits us. (vv. 11-12)

In chapter 2 I mentioned the boat trip that my friend Bruce and I took during some holidays from theological college, down the Mekong River from Chiang Khong in Thailand to Luang Prabang in Laos. Looking back, that two-day journey has been one of my travel highlights—partly because of the magnificent scenery, but mainly because of the camaraderie we enjoyed with the other backpackers. Most of our companions knew by the end of the trip that we were theological college students, and this prompted at least one spiritual discussion.

As I've travelled over the years, I've hoped that my conversations with people and my prayers for them have borne fruit for the kingdom of God. Usually you never really know whether or not this is the case, but as I was writing this chapter I thought, “Well, why not find out?” I’d kept in contact with Michael and Lynn, a couple from Northern Ireland, for a few years after the trip. They broke up several years later, but Lynn and I reconnected on Facebook and I was thrilled to learn that she had become a Christian (or returned to Christ). She’s now married, has two children, and is very involved with her local church. I decided to ask her what she remembered about our trip down the Mekong, and what she and the others made of the fact that Bruce and I were Christians. Here’s a slightly edited portion of her response:

> Hi Stephen,
> Lovely to hear from you again. I can clearly remember that boat trip. It was in a period in my life when I had strayed away from Jesus. I was fascinated to meet these two guys who were full of the joys of life, and liked travelling to discover new places as much as I did. I remember being somewhat surprised when you first said you were training to be ministers. This blew my perception of what a strong believing Christian was like completely out of the water. You seemed so normal and alive, as opposed to most of the people from my past who had a strong enough conviction to proclaim they were Christians. You seemed to get on with everyone on the boat. I know Michael loved the fact that the two of you could talk to him about sport. I’ve often thought that meeting the two of you was a pivotal point in my coming back to Christ, and giving my life to God again a few years later. You showed me what Christianity looked like in the normal world. You

> showed me Christians filled with life and joy, and that changed everything. I am now proud to say that I've shaken all my old belief systems and am happy to bring up in conversation that I'm a Christian.
> Lynn

The minefield

As I said earlier, we need to be aware when we're abroad that we are not only in a potential mission field; we're also in a potential minefield. Spending time with nonbelievers away from home, support and accountability structures leaves the way open for many temptations. If we're not walking closely with God, these temptations become even greater. To my mind three of the biggest hazards for the Christian travelling or living overseas are sexual immorality, alcohol and drugs, and alternative world views. Although we discussed some of these dangers briefly in chapter 1, we'll explore them more fully below.

Sexual immorality

In Matthew 5, Jesus says:

> "You have heard that it was said, 'You shall not commit adultery'. But I tell you that anyone who looks at a woman lustfully has already committed adultery with her in his heart." (Matt 5:27-28)

The temptation of sexual immorality is certainly not confined to life away from home, but spending time overseas with people who don't share our beliefs can heighten its danger.

Travel provides opportunities to meet lots of interesting people, and you may be physically and emotionally attracted to some of them. Being overseas can feel romantic, and people from other cultures can seem exotic. Loneliness and the thought that no-one will ever know what you've done can weaken your resolve and send your mind in unhelpful directions.

When you meet someone you find attractive, you will, if you're thinking clearly, want to act in a way that brings glory to God, and is helpful for the other person as well as for yourself. To spare yourself undue temptation and difficulty it can be wise to do things in groups. When two people who are attracted to each other start spending extended time together one-on-one, it is just so easy for them to stop thinking wisely. If you do find yourself spending time alone with a person to whom you are attracted, it's best to stick to public places—trains, cafes, common rooms, public streets, and the like. It's much harder to give in to temptation when other people are around.

But let's not just think about what we won't do in these situations; let's also think positively about what we *can* do. For a start, we can choose be a good friend to everyone we meet, including to those to whom we're attracted. If we treat them with "absolute purity" (1 Tim 5:2), these relationships can be positive, God-honouring friendships.

What about dating? Well, while there is no reason why you can't be friends with a nonbeliever to whom you're attracted, starting a romantic relationship is outrageously unwise! Dating someone who doesn't share your faith almost never ends well. My view, as I said in chapter 3, is that there's no reason to date someone unless there's a *possibility* that you *might* want to marry them at some point. A nonbeliever won't share your most important beliefs, desires and goals, so why would you marry them? Paul writes in 1 Corinthians 7:

> A woman is bound to her husband as long as he lives. But if her husband dies, she is free to marry anyone she wishes, but he must belong to the Lord. (v. 39)

If you're going to marry, marry someone who belongs to the Lord—that is, a Christian. If you're going to date, date someone who belongs to the Lord.

Temptation to sexual immorality can also come if nonbelievers you're spending time with are interested in visiting areas where the sex trade is prominent. As I noted in chapter 1, sex workers often target travellers. Even when exercising caution, I've been offered the services of men and women (including adults and children!) either directly or through intermediaries such as taxi drivers. I've seen older European men walking around with young Asian women in Bangkok, and older European women walking around with young African men in Kenya. Sex shows are mainstream in some parts of the world and very much part of the tourist trail, and pornography can be easily obtained.

It is extremely important to avoid situations where we may find ourselves genuinely tempted. With respect to the adulteress, the writer of Proverbs warns: "Keep to a path far from her" (Prov 5:8). There is no good reason to go to a sex show, to look at pornography, or to deliberately place ourselves in other tempting situations. If circumstances overtake us and we find ourselves in a situation that's threatening to get out of hand, Paul gives good advice: "Flee from sexual immorality" (1 Cor 6:18).

Alcohol and drugs

In Romans 13, Paul writes:

> Let us behave decently, as in the daytime, not in carousing and drunkenness, not in sexual immorality and debauchery, not in dissension and jealousy. (v. 13)

If you're wondering whether the Bible really understands the effect of alcohol, just look up Proverbs 23:29-35. It is well known that drunkenness and drug use causes innumerable social problems and crimes.

Drinking excessively is a socially accepted norm these days, especially on the backpacker circuit. And experimenting with illegal substances is something many young people consider to be fairly harmless. So it's highly likely that we'll face the temptation to do one or the other at some point in our travels, especially if we're spending time with people who see no reason to resist these things. Not all non-Christians will lead us towards such temptations, of course, but some will. (Sadly, so too will some Christians.)

And these dangers can be found everywhere—not just at beach parties in Thailand or Spain. Take, for example, Gili Trawangan—a small, remote island off the north-eastern coast of Lombok in Indonesia. Relatively undeveloped, with pristine beaches and turquoise waters teeming with marine life, it's something of a haven for backpackers wanting to escape the well-trodden paths of Bali. Despite Indonesia's extremely harsh drug laws, I was offered drugs on my first night on the island. (I refused.) Alcohol is also freely available there, despite the fact that this part of Indonesia is Muslim.

The Bible clearly teaches against drunkenness, and for

good reason. Being under the influence of alcohol leads to many problems, the least of which is a hangover. When we're affected by alcohol or drugs we're more likely to do something really stupid, and we're also more vulnerable to being exploited by others. When you are at home, you will often have friends looking out for you, but when you're overseas you may not have that safety net. Do you really know that Serge or Petra, people you met just the other day at the hostel, will be as vigilant and protective of your wellbeing as your long-term friends?

Alcohol and drugs are addictive, and they can lead to relational, mental, physical and financial suffering. Drinking in public is illegal in some places, and in certain countries people face very harsh criminal penalties for the possession and use of drugs. Tragically, the use of alcohol and drugs can also lead to death. In Gili Trawangan, for example, locally made spirits have caused a few fatalities because some producers bulk up their supplies with methanol.

Some of us are able to refuse alcohol or drink very little while people around us are getting smashed, but some of us cannot. Each of us needs to know our own limits. If you're unable to exercise self-control at home in your own country then there's no reason to believe you'll suddenly develop this ability overseas, and it would be wise for you to avoid alcohol altogether. And some who are self-disciplined at home may lose this capacity when they're away from home. We need to know our limits, watch ourselves carefully, check our motivations, and remain in control.

I've already described my 'maximum of two drinks a night' policy. The one time I recall bending this rule was when I had two drinks one evening and then another in the early hours of the following morning. I reasoned at the time that it was okay, given that it was a new day. Was I sticking to my rule, bending my rule, or breaking it? You be the judge. I was still in control, but it does go to show that there's always that temptation to push things further.

Alternative world views

The temptations of sex, drugs and alcohol are usually pretty obvious, and capitulation to them is fairly immediate. But the enticement of alternative world views is a different, subtler sort of danger—it's more subliminal, its impact more gradual.

I remember sitting in Bangkok Airport between flights one time, watching the world pass by. I saw suits, robes, turbans and burkas in abundance. Christians, Muslims, Buddhists, Hindus and Sikhs streamed past, no doubt along with atheists and hedonists. As I waited I found myself contemplating the great variety of belief systems on offer on our planet. I'm sure that many of the adherents I saw were devoted and sincere. Seeing this confluence of culture and religion started to work on my mind. "These people all think they're right", I pondered. "How do *I* know that Christianity is right?" Of course, I had worked through that question many times before, but there in the airport it struck me in a new way.

While I have since thought through the issue of *differing beliefs* again to my satisfaction, outcomes for others have not always been so positive. After returning from East Asia, a friend told me, "When I saw the millions of people there, I realized that if I'd been born there I would be a Buddhist. The reason I was a Christian is because I was born in Australia." This man no longer attends church or calls himself a follower of Jesus.

When we see millions of people without Christ; when we meet sincere believers from other religions who are very kind and hospitable; when we befriend engaging people for whom the resurrection of Jesus seems not only mythological but also irrelevant; we can feel overwhelmed by the weight of our questions. Different belief systems can often seem very appealing. And sometimes it can seem reasonable to conclude that they are all essentially the same, or they are all essentially wrong—or at least that none of them can claim to be the only truth. But this is why it's so important that we know *why* we believe what we believe.

Rest assured that there are clear answers to these sorts of questions, and countless Christians have worked through these issues in the past. As I said earlier, a bit of reading or research on why you believe what you believe will boost your own faith and give you confidence when talking to people with other beliefs. It's good to have an answer to questions like, "Are other religions also paths to God?"[13] It might also be helpful to familiarize yourself with the beliefs you're likely to encounter in the places you're travelling to, and to learn how they differ from Christian beliefs. There are good books and resources in this area too, including John Dickson's *A Spectator's Guide to World Religions*. You can also learn a lot from talking with Christians (missionaries and others) who have lived in those countries.

A different but related challenge that Christian travellers encounter is working out how to engage with a country's rich cultural phenomena when they integrate non-Christian

13 Again, good books and resources include Tim Keller's *The Reason for God* and Paul Little's *Know Why You Believe.*

religious practices. We might, for example, come across a beautifully designed mosque, hear a captivating Buddhist chant, or find ourselves amidst a colourful Hindu festival.

Paul's response to the 'enriching cultural phenomena' of this sort in Athens, as we read in Acts 17, is instructive:

> While Paul was waiting for them in Athens, he was greatly distressed to see that the city was full of idols. (v. 16)

He is distressed, but he doesn't simply dwell on his emotion. He responds in a constructive way, as we see in the following verse:

> So he reasoned in the synagogue with both Jews and God-fearing Greeks, as well as in the marketplace day by day with those who happened to be there. (v. 17)

Furthermore, he has familiarized himself with the local beliefs, and is able to put his knowledge to good use not long afterwards:

> Paul then stood up in the meeting of the Areopagus and said: "People of Athens! I see that in every way you are very religious. For as I walked around and looked carefully at your objects of worship, I even found an altar with this inscription: TO AN UNKNOWN GOD. So you are ignorant of the very thing you worship—and this is what I am going to proclaim to you." (vv. 22-23)

It would be fair to say that other belief systems contain many worthy principles, and have inspired some impressive music, artwork and architecture. Millions of people are sincerely committed to these religions. But at their core these belief systems are false, and ultimately they will not do anyone any good. The best response is to recognize and appreciate whatever is admirable or worthy in such faiths, to love the people devoted to them, and to prayerfully try to point them towards Christ.

I once visited Wat Pho—an impressive Buddhist temple complex in Bangkok, and home to a famous reclining Buddha. Architecturally, Wat Pho is fascinating. And I'm sure that many of the devotees who visit are lovely people. But I was filled with sadness as I watched many expressing their commitment to this non-Christian belief. As I walked around the site with another backpacker, a nonbeliever, I discovered that he was interested in hearing and talking about the death and resurrection of Jesus, and its implications for us. Exposure to various forms of religious expression can sometimes prompt this kind of conversation.

Some encouragement: the unknown backpacker

As I was writing this book I caught up with an old friend for coffee, who told me that a few years ago she'd re-established contact with a childhood friend of hers named Fiona. Fiona had recently been diagnosed with cancer, so my friend went to visit her in hospital. During their time together, my friend nervously asked if she could read John's Gospel with her and pray with her. Fiona welcomed the idea.

As the two women chatted, Fiona recalled a time in her twenties when she and another friend were backpacking around Europe and the United States. At a youth hostel somewhere on that trip, a fellow backpacker had shared

Christ with them. Fiona remembered that what she heard had a strong impact on her, but at the time she'd reasoned that there would be time later in life for God. But Fiona never forgot that conversation, and 25 years later, in his mercy, God used the influence of that unknown backpacker, as well as my friend and others, to help Fiona become a Christian not long before she went home to be with the God who was now her Lord.

Never underestimate the ways in which God can use your efforts to share the good news of Jesus!

Checklist for connecting with non-Christians

- Resolve to travel with God—spend time with him regularly, and track down Christian fellowship.
- Resolve to live as a Christian—be prepared to resist temptation, and seek to live in a godly way.
- Pray that God would lead you to nonbelievers to whom you can witness.
- Know *what* you believe—learn a gospel outline so that you can explain it to someone.
- Know *why* you believe it and think through how you'd answer commonly asked questions.
- Consider taking a Christian tract or booklet with you that you can give to people when the opportunity arises.
- Include references to God, Jesus, Christianity and church naturally in your everyday conversations. For example, when people ask what you do, you could mention something 'Christian' in your answer; "...and I also teach Sunday School on weekends" or "I play football in a team with some friends from church".

- Consider leaving conversation-starters (like your Bible or a Christian book) lying around—or at least don't hide them away.
- Research the spiritual beliefs of the countries you'll be visiting.
- Expect that you will be tempted to do *none* of the things suggested in this checklist. Don't let sin ruin your time abroad—or your life.

5

TRAVELLING IN A FALLEN WORLD

"Their mouths are full of cursing and bitterness."
"Their feet are swift to shed blood;
ruin and misery mark their ways,
and the way of peace they do not know."
"There is no fear of God before their eyes."
(Rom 3:14-18)

The name is synonymous with horror: Auschwitz. This network of concentration and extermination camps in southern Poland was responsible for the deaths of more than a million people—mostly Jews—during the Second World War. The Germans ran them with ruthless efficiency. If the prisoners weren't killed by the gas chambers or by execution, they stood the risk of dying from starvation, overwork, disease or medical experimentation. The inhumanity and depravity of the place is barely conceivable.

It was an overcast day when I caught the train from

Kraków to the town of Oświęcim to visit Auschwitz I and Auschwitz II-Birkenau, which are now maintained as museums. I started at Auschwitz I, the original camp, where I saw various exhibitions with headings like 'Extermination', 'Everyday Life of the Prisoner', 'Suffering and Struggle of the Jews', and 'The "Death Block"'. Head shots of victims were displayed in the thousands, along with collections of personal items such as suitcases, shoes, eyeglasses, hair and artificial limbs. Visitors can walk to the gallows, the 'wall of death', the gas chamber and the crematorium. The infamous sign proclaiming 'Arbeit macht frei' ('Work brings freedom') remains over the main gate. In a small cinema I watched a short film taken by the Russian Army in 1945 when they liberated the camp.

The mood everywhere was sombre and focused, and I spoke quietly with other visitors as we tried to absorb the depth of this horror together. Some backpackers and I decided to walk the two kilometres to the Auschwitz II-Birkenau site. It was something of a relief to have others with whom to talk and process things. Birkenau was enormous. The train lines stretching into the camp were still there, as were a few of what must have been hundreds of barracks. The misery and magnitude of the place was impossible to grasp. Later that night, as I sat in a smoky train carriage reflecting on the day and penning a few thoughts in my diary, I noted a deeper appreciation for Corrie ten Boom.

The darkness

While the world is an amazing place, it's also a very, very dark place. We live in a fallen world, as passages such as

Genesis 3 and Romans 1-3 make clear. Jesus said, "This is the verdict: Light has come into the world, but people loved darkness instead of light because their deeds were evil" (John 3:19). And it shows. The earth is devastatingly scarred by sin, by the effects of human rebellion against God.

Jesus often grieved over the state of the world. He wept at the tomb of Lazarus (John 11:35), felt anguish at the hypocrisy of the Jewish religious leaders (Matt 23:1-36), expressed outrage at the exploitation in the temple (Mark 11:15-17), and lamented Jerusalem's resistance to God (Luke 13:34). If we're walking closely with God, we'll experience similar emotions as we survey our surroundings.

Most of us are probably familiar to some extent with the darkness in our home countries, but overseas we'll encounter whole new dimensions of black. You don't have to wander too far from the tourist traps to find sad and often appalling realities. In fact, if you look carefully around even the plushest resort you'll find human tragedy there as well.

Sometimes the harsh truths of our fallen world will walk right across your path, as when a drug addict persistently harassed me for money in Amsterdam. At other times you might deliberately seek them out, as when I visited Auschwitz on that chilly Polish day. Why visit a place like Auschwitz? It depends on why you're travelling. If you're abroad solely for leisure, you may avoid such places. But if one of your reasons for travelling is to learn about God's world and about humanity, you might include places like this in your itinerary.

Preparation

Christians who travel and live overseas can have their emotions and sometimes even their faith buffeted by the horrors to which they're exposed. How could God allow Auschwitz? What about those who live, suffer and die in slums around the world? These are good questions, and determining a biblical response will help us to be prepared when we encounter these realities close up.

Suffering and evil—whether at home or abroad—should not surprise the Christian. In Mark 13, Jesus says to his disciples, "So be on your guard; I have told you everything ahead of time" (v. 23). In this chapter of Mark's Gospel, Jesus speaks in general terms about the calamities that will take place in the time prior to his return—that is, I believe, the period between Jesus' first and second comings—the time in which we're now living. Jesus gives this warning in part so that his followers will be prepared, and won't be taken by surprise when the disasters described in Mark 13 come to pass.

Our journeys overseas may take us directly or indirectly (e.g. via museums, memorials and stories) into the presence of poverty, political unrest, war, genocide, the sex industry, the drug industry, racism, spiritual need, false religion, false 'Christian' teaching, and religious persecution. This is to say nothing of all the 'everyday' interpersonal sins that we find the world over.

The best preparation for all this is to ensure that we're walking closely with God. This will enable our thinking—the way we view and respond to the world—to be more in sync with God's. It is also helpful, as I've said, to know *what* we believe and *why* we believe it. The fallenness of the world in which we travel will undoubtedly raise intellectual and emotional questions about our faith, so a clear understanding of the gospel and a basic grasp of apologetics will be of immeasurable value. Thanks to good Bible teaching at my church, helpful discussions with other believers, and stimulating Christian books, I was fortunate to have much of this groundwork in place before I first set off to England as a 20-year-old.

Anyone travelling to the developing world, as I did on my second trek into foreign parts, will benefit from thinking beforehand about what the Bible has to say about suffering. What is the reason for suffering? What, if anything, has God done about suffering? What's the appropriate human response to suffering? As we come face to face with poverty, famine and slums, these questions can seem overwhelming.

Different cultures and people understand and respond to suffering in different ways. Traditionally, many Africans have had a simple explanation for suffering: witchcraft! Why did that baby die? Witchcraft. What should we do in response? Find out who cast the spell. Most Westerners will dismiss this sort of explanation and response, but what do they put in its place?

In the face of suffering on a grand scale—for example, famine and genocide—we may be tempted to conclude that God is weak, or doesn't care, or doesn't exist, or is a moral monster. Thankfully, there are lots of good resources that will help prevent us from falling into this sort of trap, including John Dickson's *If I Were God, I'd End All the Pain* and Don Carson's *How Long, O Lord?*, as well as Tim Keller's *The Reason for God* and Paul Little's *Know Why You Believe*.

Given that the question of suffering can be so personal

and emotionally intense, and can come up for so many different reasons, I would suggest wrestling with the topic in some depth with an open Bible and one or more of the resources I've listed above. That said, a few brief comments here may be of some help.

Suffering was not originally part of God's creation (Genesis 1-2). It came into the world because of human sin (Genesis 3; Rom 5:12, 6:23, 8:18-23). But suffering is not proportional to merit—some people suffer much more than others, and we don't know why (Luke 13:1-5). The Bible doesn't answer this question for us. But we do know that God has suffered and understands suffering (Heb 2:18, 4:15; Job); that he helps us deal with suffering (Pss 34:19, 46:1); that he comforts us in our suffering (Ps 23:4); that he can use suffering for good (Gen 50:20; Rom 8:28; Heb 12:11). And we know that he will eventually eliminate suffering forever (Revelation 21-22).

I've found comfort and reassurance in the following verses when I've dealt with suffering at close range. Psalm 34 tells us that "The Lord is close to the brokenhearted and saves those who are crushed in spirit" (v. 18). Jesus reassures us that "even the very hairs of your head are all numbered" (Matt 10:30). God knows me better than I know myself. And Hebrews 4 encourages us with the truth that Jesus is able to "empathize with our weaknesses" and that he "has been tempted in every way, just as we are—yet he did not sin" (v. 15).

I would also add that I find the Bible's teaching on suffering far more appealing and helpful than my understanding of the teaching on suffering that is offered by Hinduism, Buddhism, Islam and atheism.

In conclusion, you might say that Jesus suffered to help end suffering. As John 3:16 reassures us:

> For God so loved the world that he gave his one and only Son, that whoever believes in him shall not perish but have eternal life.

Forearming ourselves with a mature appreciation of the Bible's teaching on suffering will help us to survive rather than sink when we come face to face with it.

Poverty

Aside from my short stopover at Madras (Chennai) Airport en route to London, my first real exposure to poverty was in Zimbabwe, where the materially deprived were found everywhere—from the slums of the city to the villages in the countryside. The tragic scarcity of life's basics was impossible to ignore. Poverty is a worldwide phenomenon, found even in the richest of countries, but it is particularly prevalent in the developing world.

The Mathare slums in Nairobi are home to roughly half a million people. Residents live with unemployment, crime, garbage, raw sewage, ramshackle housing, and disease. Having visited and preached in a church there a number of times, I now have some familiarity with the area. The church building is made of corrugated iron, and sits on a road that's constantly covered with litter. But despite its surroundings, the fellowship is welcoming and warm, and these believers engage in good Christian ministry, including aid and development work. In even the bleakest environment, Christ can bring hope. And sometimes the bleaker the environment, the brighter Christ's hope shines.

Disease is poverty's close companion. People going to Africa and other parts of the developing world will be aware of this because of all the injections and pills they need to take prior to travelling. Many will take antimalarial tablets, for example—and for good reason. The World Health Organization reports that there were almost 400,000 deaths from malaria in Africa in 2015.[14] HIV is also prevalent. The Joint United Nations Programme on HIV/AIDS advises that in Sub-Saharan Africa in 2013, an estimated 24.7 million people were living with HIV.[15] But the situation isn't entirely without hope, and governments, NGOs and Christian organizations are taking steps to alleviate HIV/AIDS. I have links with two Christian groups in Nairobi who are doing very good work in this area.

But it's one thing to note statistics and another thing to get to know the people involved. My friends Stephen and Rosemary, a Kenyan couple, are both heavily involved in Christian ministry in Africa. Rosemary recently wrote a short autobiography of her life, and because I've only known her as a warm, educated and ministry-minded adult, I was somewhat shocked to read about her childhood.

Rosemary's parents separated when she was young, and she was raised by her mother. They lived in a small, grass-thatched hut with dirty walls. The family's goats slept inside

14 World Health Organization, 'Fact Sheet: World Malaria Report 2015', WHO, Geneva, updated edn, 19 April 2016 (viewed 23 December 2016): www.who.int/malaria/media/world-malaria-report-2015/en/.

15 Joint United Nations Programme on HIV/AIDS (UNAIDS), *The Gap Report*, updated edn, Geneva, Switzerland, September 2014, p. 26 (viewed 23 December 2016): www.unaids.org/sites/default/files/media_asset/UNAIDS_Gap_report_en.pdf.

with them, which gave the place a smell of dung and urine. When the family moved to a small, single-room dwelling in the city, they had to use old newspapers to block cracks in the wall. This room was their living room, bedroom and bathroom. Their toilet, if they could not sneak into their neighbour's pit latrine, was either the nearby river or a plastic bag that was thrown out of the house at night. This one room housed seven children, including Rosemary and her siblings and other relatives.

Most of the families in the neighbourhood were headed by single mothers whose primary sources of income were prostitution and brewing gin, although some managed to find jobs as waitresses or cleaners. With the dwellings packed so closely together there was a distinct lack of privacy, and from a very young age Rosemary was exposed to sexual immorality, abortion, alcohol abuse and physical violence.

Rosemary's mother worked nights in bars and restaurants. She was ill-tempered and began drinking heavily. Despite this, she worked hard and did her best to raise her children. This involved the regular use of beatings as a disciplinary method. Rosemary's mother died when Rosemary was 21. Despite her mother's shortcomings, Rosemary remembers her as someone who was diligent, courageous, prudent, hospitable, and dedicated to the education of her children.[16]

Stories like this are common in Africa. Thankfully, Rosemary's life turned around entirely. She became a Christian when she was a teenager and did well in her studies, and she's now married with two children. She has a

16 To read more of Rosemary's story, see Rosemary W Mbogo, *Against All Odds: Rising Up from a Humble Beginning*, Utafiti Foundation, Eldoret, 2015.

PhD from an American university and works as a university lecturer in Nairobi. With her husband, she has pastored a church and set up and run various development projects, a children's home, and a school. Unfortunately, many stories do not turn out like Rosemary's but end instead in sudden tragedy or after prolonged misery.

It will come as no surprise to learn that whenever I'm in Africa, people ask me for money—and have done so from my very first full day there. At first, as a budget backpacker, part of me stupidly thought, "Hey, I've only just finished studying full-time. I don't have a job yet. I'm travelling on a budget. I'm not like the rich tourists you see at the Hilton." I suspect this was a distinction most locals wouldn't have appreciated, though. As far as they were concerned, I was white and my shoes didn't have holes in them—so I was rich. And, of course, I was.

On that first trip to Africa I developed a strategy for dealing with these requests. I couldn't hand out cash to everyone who asked or I would soon have been broke. So instead of handing out cash, I decided to donate money to Christian organizations that were doing aid and development work in Africa. I figured this would be a more effective use of my money. Having said that, when I've been travelling on public transport and have struck up some sort of relationship with a fellow passenger, I've sometimes offered to buy them a drink or a sandwich or share some of my food with them.

Financial scams are common in Africa, as they are in other parts of the world. Westerners are often the targets of bogus requests for money for such things as 'Christian ministry' or 'medical treatment'. These appeals are often made online. Never trust an online request for money from someone you don't know—no matter the reason, no matter how heart-rending the appeal.

While suffering can seem overwhelming, we aren't powerless in the face of it. There *are* things we can do. We can pray, and we can support organizations that work to prevent and respond to suffering in its various forms. My practice has usually been to provide prayer and financial assistance to Christian mission agencies, Christian aid and development organizations and, in a very limited number of situations, to individuals. Supporting Christian mission—by which I mean evangelism, discipleship and supporting ministries—is crucial, because the spread of the gospel can transform lives and society (thus reducing suffering), to say nothing of securing people's eternal inheritance. Supporting Christian aid and development is also important as this work helps prevent suffering and responds in situation-specific ways to significant forms of suffering. You might also decide to work with a Christian mission group and/or an aid and development organization at some point in the future. If this interests you, you may want to visit some of these organizations during your time overseas.

War and political unrest

I have always sought to avoid 'active' war and situations of political unrest in my travels. While I'm all for adventure, I find nothing appealing or admirable about pointlessly risking one's life for the sake of some cheap adrenalin rush. When I was first in Africa, there was an overland route from Zimbabwe to Malawi that took you through Mozambique for about 150 kilometres. Mozambique was then in a state of civil war, and the journey could only be taken with an army convoy. The exact statistics now elude me, but something like, say, one in 20 or one in 50 convoys were attacked. Some backpackers saw this trip as an adventure. I considered it a ridiculous backpacking version of Russian roulette. There may be times when there's some very good reason to risk our lives, but for me it will need to be for something better than having a good tale to tell. If you want an adrenalin rush, do a bungee jump!

Even if we take care to avoid areas of active military conflict, our travels will often bring us into more indirect contact with the horrors of war. When a friend and I finished two weeks of theological lecturing in south-western Uganda, we were so close to Rwanda that we decided to hop across the border for a day or two before returning to Australia. So, late one sunny afternoon, having negotiated the crowds and queues at passport control and customs, we met our local contact. There were handshakes and smiles all round, and in the course of our introductory chitchat I asked him about his family and how many children he had.

"Oh, one of my own and 33 others", he said. My mind quickly unpacked his response. The Rwandan genocide had occurred 15 years earlier. This man and his wife must have been looking after the children of deceased relatives and friends.

The genocide of 1994 put this small African country on the world map for all the wrong reasons. It is estimated that up to a million Rwandans—about 70% of the Tutsi tribe, and 20% of the country's total population—were killed over a 100-day period from April to June. It came as a shock to many that something like this could still happen in our increasingly interconnected world. It's even more shocking when we consider that the majority of the country's citizens considered themselves to be Christians.

We stayed the night in the capital, Kigali. The next afternoon we visited the Kigali Genocide Memorial Centre, where we learned about the Rwandan tragedy as well as genocides in other countries over the preceding century. Perhaps most sobering of all was the fact that the centre, which is about the size of a primary school, contains the interred remains of a quarter of a million victims.

As Christians, we shouldn't be surprised by the prevalence and brutality of war. The Scriptures teach that we should expect this, and history reminds us that such atrocities have been taking place since time immemorial. In Mark 13:7, Jesus says, "When you hear of wars and rumours of wars, do not be alarmed. Such things must happen, but the end is still to come". And Romans 3 contains Paul's blunt assessment of humanity:

> "Their mouths are full of cursing and bitterness."
> "Their feet are swift to shed blood;
> ruin and misery mark their ways,
> and the way of peace they do not know."
> "There is no fear of God before their eyes."
> (vv. 14-18)

The sex industry and the drug industry

As we've discussed, the vast majority of people who go abroad will come across opportunities to indulge in sexual immorality and illegal drug use. But these encounters are only the tip of the iceberg. They merely represent the retail end of industries dominated by callous criminal empires.

The sex industry is a depressingly lucrative one. The red-light districts in many cities have become major tourist attractions, exemplifying the depressing scenario that Paul describes in Romans 1:

> Although they know God's righteous decree that those who do such things deserve death, they not only continue to do these very things but also approve of those who practise them. (v. 32)

Amsterdam's red-light district, known as De Wallen, has found its way onto the official and unofficial itineraries of many travellers and tour groups. When I was in Amsterdam, I deliberately avoided this section of the city. If you are male, and think that it would be good as a Christian to be better informed about this sort of problem, and so decide one night that you might go and take a look at the place for yourself, could I suggest that you may be deluding yourself as to your motives.

It has been reported that about 75% of Amsterdam's prostitutes are from Eastern Europe, Africa and Asia.[17] It comes as no surprise, then, to learn that the Netherlands has a particular problem with human trafficking.[18] Similar comments could be made about the sex industry's links with organized crime and

17 In Karina Schaapman's 2008 report about the Amsterdam sex trade, referred to in Marlise Simons, 'Amsterdam Tries Upscale Fix for Red-Light District Crime', *The New York Times*, 24 February 2008 (viewed 28 January 2017): www.nytimes.com/2008/02/24/world/europe/24amsterdam.html.

18 Publications Office of the European Union, *Trafficking in Human Beings*, Eurostat Statistical Working Papers, European Union, Luxembourg, 2014, pp. 11, 34-5 (viewed 23 December 2016): www.ec.europa.eu/anti-trafficking/sites/antitrafficking/files/trafficking_in_human_beings_-_eurostat_-_2014_edition.pdf.

human trafficking elsewhere in the world.

Illegal drugs are also widely available around the globe. Again, vast criminal empires lie behind their production and distribution, generating hundreds of billions of dollars each year. The criminals get rich as millions upon millions of lives are ruined.

One afternoon in Amsterdam, I was walking to the Van Gogh Museum when I was confronted by a guy in his twenties asking for money for food. Sizing him up, I concluded that he did not actually want to buy food. He was articulate, threatening and persistent. Our conversation went something like this:

"Hey, could you give me some money for some food?"

"Sorry, no, mate."

"Well, what am I going to do? I'm hungry."

Assuming that a place such as Amsterdam would have soup kitchens and the like, I said, "I'm sure there are places where you can go to get something to eat".

"What places? There aren't any." (I confirmed later that, of course, there are.)

"Well, I think there are and I'm not giving you any money."

"I'm desperate. And I'm going to keep on talking until you give me some."

"You can do that if you want to, but I'm not going to give you anything."

All this time I was trying to walk away from him, but he kept following. "I don't like you very much", he said. "How do you know I'm not going to follow you around a corner and take your money by force?"

I was bigger than he was, but he might have had a knife or a syringe. By this stage I was in a state of high alert. "Well, I don't think you should do that. But I'm not giving you anything, so you may as well give up."

I made sure I kept walking along very public streets, the exchanges continued, and eventually—eventually—he did give up and go away. On one level, the dialogue had a slightly comic feel—but here was a clearly intelligent and articulate guy reduced to begging for money to support his habit.

Drug addiction of a different sort can be seen on the streets of Nairobi. Walking around the central business district there, I've seen many children with filthy clothes and vacant expressions. Here in the Kenyan capital, street children sniff glue. The *Voice of America* website reports that, according to one estimate, over half of the city's 50,000 street children are addicted to the stuff. The children sniff glue because of peer pressure, to feel good from the high, to stay warm, and to ward off hunger pains. The glue they sniff is normally used to repair things like shoes and upholstery. Inhaling can lead to addiction and victims may stop eating and lose weight. Some eventually die. To finance their habit, these children may resort to scavenging, begging, stealing and prostitution.[19]

Racism

Racism is a prejudice or animosity toward people of another race, and travelling will expose you to many examples of it. You will find it in others. You will perhaps find traces of it in yourself. It is not the sole province of any one racial group or area—on every continent, ethnic and tribal conflicts abound.

19 Cathy Majtenyi, 'Study: Glue-Sniffing Epidemic Rampant Among Kenyan Street Children', *Voice of America*, 1 November 2009 (viewed 23 December 2016): www.voanews.com/a/a-13-2008-12-01-voa48/404787.html.

Racism can range from milder forms of interpersonal prejudice through to genocide, apartheid, and other forms of segregation and violence.

The Rwandan genocide was a manifestation of racism at its most extreme, but seemingly milder forms of racism are also very damaging. In one country I visited, I was particularly embarrassed by the way in which some Westerners treated indigenous service staff. Racist attitudes often simmer below the surface. I visited Kenya four times between 2003 and 2006 and felt I had some understanding of the country and its people. But I was shocked when, after the country's 2007 election, violence broke out along tribal lines.

There is no place for racism among Christians. All people are created by God and are equal before him. For Christians, as Paul writes in Galatians 3, "There is neither Jew nor Gentile, neither slave nor free, nor is there male and female, for you are all one in Christ Jesus" (v. 28). Not once in all of my trips to Africa to teach theology have I detected even the faintest feeling of resentment from any of my hosts or students based on my skin colour. I've always been treated with kindness and hospitality.

Some have suggested that travel itself can often work against racism. As the 19th-century American writer Mark Twain wisely said, "Travel is fatal to prejudice, bigotry and narrow-mindedness, and many of our people need it sorely on these accounts".[20]

20 Mark Twain, *The Innocents Abroad*, General Books, Memphis, 2010, p. 325.

Spiritual drought

In the previous chapter we discussed the spiritual needs that we'll find wherever we go, and the fact that some people are quite open to hearing the good news about Jesus. Across the globe there's an overwhelming need for the gospel. In some countries, such as those in the Middle East that are dominated by Islam, there's little awareness of the gospel. My only experience of this part of the world has been a few days in Dubai, the largest city in the United Arab Emirates. While I understand that the United Arab Emirates is far less restrictive concerning Christianity than other countries in the region, proselytizing is illegal and conversion from Islam is discouraged.[21]

In some countries, like those in Europe, there is a feeling of having moved beyond the gospel, resulting in a strongly secular culture. Many beautiful old church buildings are used more as sites for concerts and other cultural activities than for active church life. Even in Australia, England and the United Sates, there's a fairly hostile form of atheism developing that seems to want to shut down any discussion at all about religion. In my view, people have the right to freedom of belief with respect to religion, whether it be Christianity, atheism or any other form of belief. I also feel that when discussion or debate takes place between people of differing beliefs, it should be done in a respectful and reasoned way. Unfortunately, this is not how many public interactions on these issues take place these days.

21 Voice of the Martyrs, *2017 Global Report on Where Christians Are Persecuted Today*, Voice of the Martyrs, Lawson, NSW, 2017, p. 27 (viewed 16 June 2017): www.vom.com.au/wp-content/uploads/2017/05/Global-Report-2017_au.pdf.

In other countries, such as those in Sub-Saharan Africa, while there may be a high rate of church attendance, "Christianity in Africa is a mile wide and an inch deep" (as one Kenyan Christian leader told me). Rwanda, for example, was a 'Christian country' at the time of the genocide, but clearly the faith of many had not sunk very deep. One Rwandan Christian leader told me that Rwandan churches were good at evangelism but less focused on discipleship. They could preach the good news of Christ, but they didn't then teach new Christians how to live as followers of Christ.

Many churches in Sub-Saharan Africa are led by fine Christian people, but many are led by people who haven't had the opportunity (or sometimes perhaps the inclination) to sufficiently familiarize themselves with the Scriptures. As a result, poor teaching is rife. Some 'churches' are more like cults, and tragedies have resulted. Jesus warns, "For false messiahs and false prophets will appear and perform signs and wonders to deceive, if possible, even the elect" (Mark 13:22). One example of this occurred in the settlement of Kanungu, not far from where I've taught theology in south-western Uganda. In March 2000, hundreds of members of the Movement for the Restoration of the Ten Commandments of God descended upon Kanungu. The cult's leaders had told its members that the Virgin Mary had appeared to the leaders and informed them that the world would end on 17 March 2000. So on that date, the members held a huge party and then arrived at the church to pray and sing. They were told that the Virgin Mary would come to them personally, clothed in flames, to take them to heaven. The building was lit and flames engulfed the structure, killing the 530 people inside. Around the same time, about 400 other members of the movement were found dead elsewhere in the country. By anyone's definition, this was 'religion gone wrong'.

The great needs around the world for evangelism, good teaching and discipleship should remind us that Jesus' Great Commission in Matthew 28:19-20 remains a priority for all Christians:

> "Therefore go and make disciples of all nations, baptizing them in the name of the Father and of the Son and of the Holy Spirit, and teaching them to obey everything I have commanded you. And surely I am with you always, to the very end of the age."

What would it mean for you—in terms of your prayers, money, time and ministry—to prioritize the Great Commission?

Christian persecution

I haven't had much personal exposure to the persecution of Christians in other countries, partly because I haven't visited those countries where it is at its worst. The Christian organization Open Doors publishes a 'World Watch List'—a yearly ranking of the top 50 countries where the persecution of Christians is most intense. Looking through the list for 2016 I realized that I've only visited seven of the 50: Kenya (ranked 16), India (17), Ethiopia (18), Vietnam (20), Laos (29), Indonesia (43) and the United Arab Emirates (47). In these countries, opposition tends to come from Muslims, Hindus and communists. The fact that Kenya has such a high ranking may surprise some since most Kenyans would describe themselves as Christian, but it's the terrorist activities conducted inside its borders by the Somali Islamic terrorist group Al-Shabaab that place this country so high on the list.[22]

The persecution of Christians in these seven countries wasn't that obvious to me as a casual traveller. As I mentioned in chapter 4, I only learned of the extent of the persecution of Christians in Vietnam after I'd returned to Australia. India is probably the country where I most sensed the opposition to Christianity. Only a few weeks before I attended the Maramon Christian Convention in southern India, Graham Staines, an Australian missionary, had been burned to death along with his two young sons by some hardline Hindus in the east of the country. I got the impression during my visit that this weighed heavily on the hearts and minds of many Indian Christians.

The extent to which Christians are persecuted around the globe is disturbing, but it shouldn't be surprising. The Bible warns us many times that persecution will be the lot of those who follow Jesus. Jesus speaks of it (e.g. Mark 13:9), as does Paul: "In fact, everyone who wants to live a godly life in Christ Jesus will be persecuted" (2 Tim 3:12).

Our response

As we prepare for travelling in a fallen world, we need to work on our relationship with God, and understand what we believe and why we believe it. It will also be helpful to gain a deeper understanding of the biblical view of suffering. But,

22 'World Watch List: Country Profiles', Open Doors Australia, Castle Hill, NSW, 2016 (viewed 23 December 2016): www.opendoors.org.au/persecuted-christians/world-watch-list/.

in addition to *preparing*, there are also lots of positive things we can do to *respond*.

We can seek to live as Christians when we're abroad, responding positively and biblically to people and situations. While we're away and when we return home, we can pray for and financially support Christian mission agencies and development organizations. We can also pray for and financially support individuals and groups with whom we've had personal contact. We might also consider moving into full-time or part-time ministry in one of these areas.

It's encouraging to see how a deeper understanding of the Scriptures can help to alleviate suffering. Patience was a keen student in the first two-week theology course I ever taught in Africa. Part way through the course, once the students and I had gotten to know each other, she asked me whether I thought Jesus would want to help people who were suffering from AIDS. I said that, based on his example in the New Testament, these were exactly the sorts of people Jesus would want to help, and that he also would have spent time with them. Then I asked her why she'd raised the question.

"Here in Kenya", she told me, "many think that AIDS is the judgement of God". The implication seemed to be that we should leave the victims of AIDS to 'reap what they had sown' and do nothing to help them. I expressed my very strong disagreement with this attitude, and wrote her a page or two explaining my understanding of the biblical teaching on sin, judgement, suffering, and helping those in need.

Patience has since gone on to set up a ministry for people suffering from HIV/AIDS and their families. It points those who are affected towards Christ; and provides them with a supportive community, counseling and other practical assistance. I've prayed for this work and supported it financially in a modest way. The last time I was in Nairobi I visited the ministry, met about 30 people who were being helped, and was invited to give a short Christian talk.

When we seek to walk closely with God in this fallen world, with all its great needs, he can guide us into situations where, even in humble ways, he uses us to make a difference.

Checklist for travelling in a fallen world

- Resolve to travel with God—spend time with him regularly, and track down Christian fellowship.
- Prepare yourself for exposure to the darkness you'll encounter overseas by making sure you know *what* you believe as a Christian and *why* you believe it. In particular, make sure you know what the Bible teaches about the fallen nature of the world and about suffering (perhaps with the assistance of one of the books I've recommended).
- Try to respond prayerfully and biblically to the darkness you encounter—while you're abroad and also when you return home. Consider which people, places or organizations you could pray for and/or financially support.
- Expect that you will be tempted to do *none* of the things suggested in this checklist. Don't let sin ruin your time abroad—or your life.

6

HOW TO TRAVEL

For by the grace given me I say to every one of you: Do not think of yourself more highly than you ought, but rather think of yourself with sober judgement, in accordance with the faith God has distributed to each one of you. (Rom 12:3)

I still remember the clipping that my mother—an inveterate cutter-outer of relevant newspaper articles—left on my desk when I was 20, not long before I left for my five-month cricket stint in London. It was a piece of travel writing, a genre to which I had previously given very little thought. But since it was gradually dawning on me that going to London was, in fact, *travel*, and not just a step on the path towards becoming a professional cricketer, travel articles were now of interest.

As I recall, the journalist was reflecting upon a seminal childhood trip away from home. Just before she left, her mother had pressed a penny into her hand and said, "The world is your oyster". For some reason I found the phrase highly evocative. The world is your oyster. The words stuck in my head, stirring in me a sense of excitement and possibility.

These days travel writing abounds. You can read about the travels of other people, and about the trips other people think you should do. You can also pick up some very good advice from books, articles and blogs about *how* to travel or *how* to live overseas. They might advise you to travel light, to get off the beaten track, to meet the locals, not to rush, how to travel with another person, how to travel alone, how to live overseas, to take basic safety precautions, what to do about money, and so on.

But while much travel writing contains sound, common-sense counsel, very little is written from a Christian perspective—so it won't *all* be good advice. Most travel writing assumes that God is totally irrelevant to your time away. Few writers address what God's word has to say on the decisions we make about travelling and living overseas (the topic of this chapter). It's also rare to find travel writing that considers how the Scriptures might help us think through whether we should travel or live overseas at all (the topic of the next chapter). Some travel writing gives advice that a Christian should clearly recognize as bad advice, like the online piece I read that promoted the value of short-term romantic relationships on the road—liaisons that might last anything from a few weeks to a few months, as travel and life plans permit.

During the time I've spent reflecting on my own experiences and on those of other believers, I've become convinced that it's crucial for us to address the 'How to travel and live abroad' questions from a Christian perspective.

There are three main considerations:

1. How will the nature of my trip or overseas living arrangements affect my relationship with God?
2. What sort of trip or overseas living arrangement suits my personality, state of health and gender?
3. What sort of trip or overseas living arrangement constitutes a wise use of my money and time?

We'll address the third question, which is about Christian stewardship, in chapter 7. In this chapter we'll focus on the first and second questions, which are both fundamentally about knowing yourself.

Know thyself

How do you see yourself? In those moments of quiet reflection, when you contemplate your identity, your personality, your strengths and your weaknesses... what do you come up with? At a dinner party I attended many years ago, we decided to play a dangerous game. The idea was to mention a person's name—it might be a famous person, it might be someone who was at the dinner party—and a nominated person at the table then had to say the first thing that came into their head.

The game began. A few names were suggested and responses given. And then it happened—someone called out "Stephen Liggins". The person who had to answer was an old school friend, a girl who remains to this day a good friend to my wife and me. What would she say? Undercover superhero? Renaissance man? Reluctant heartthrob? Cultural bohemian? Quick as a flash, she blurted out, "Disciplined".

Disciplined? Me? Of all the things she could have said, that was what she came out with?!? I think it took us all by surprise. This wasn't normally the first thing that jumped into my head when I thought of myself, but as I think back on it I realize how insightful she was. I am disciplined. I'm the sort of person who tends to stick at things, to finish what I start. While I'm far from perfect, when it comes to living as a Christian I regularly have my quiet times, and I generally maintain certain standards when it comes to language, alcohol, honesty, and the treatment of others. The fact that others around me may think or act very differently tends to have little impact on me.

Over the years I've learned that many others (believers and nonbelievers), while possessing fine qualities I lack, are not as disciplined as I am. Situations that don't have a negative impact on me, therefore, may negatively affect others. When I'm travelling and utterly out of my routine, I will generally still have my quiet times. When I'm surrounded by people who are getting drunk, I will remain sober. I certainly have my failings—I am no superhero—but the Holy Spirit, working through a combination of genetics and upbringing, has made me disciplined.

Thinking about my time in London as a young man, and the extremely positive spiritual experience I had, I now realize that many things were working in my favour. In addition to my disciplined nature, I'd already been a keen Christian for around ten years; I was from a Christian family; I was involved in a good church; I'd had a lot of experience being a Christian in non-Christian contexts (for example, as part of sporting teams and university social life); I was convinced that living the Christian way was much better than the alternatives; and people were praying for me. Finally, when told about a good church, I went along to it and got involved.

What do you have working in your favour as you think about travelling overseas? Let me encourage you, as you think about these things, to know thyself! Paul writes in Romans 12:3:

> For by the grace given me I say to every one of you: Do not think of yourself more highly than you ought, but rather think of yourself with sober judgement, in accordance with the faith God has distributed to each of you.

One more thing—and I can't stress this enough: it would be very helpful to ask an older, wiser Christian whom you respect, and who knows you well, to give you their insights on what they think might and might not be helpful for your Christian life as you travel. We sometimes make inaccurate and unrealistic assessments of ourselves, and this sort of loving assistance can help us to plan wisely.

A good dose of self-knowledge is invaluable as we move on to consider some of the common 'How to travel' questions. We need to think about these issues most importantly in light of how they might affect our relationship with God, as well as in terms of how the people we travel with, the pace of travel, the budget, and so on will suit our personality and circumstances.

Going solo or with a friend

The important question here is how going solo or with a friend will affect your relationship with God. How will it affect your quiet times? Will you seek out Christian fellowship while you're away? How will travelling with or without a companion affect your behaviour when you're with people who aren't believers and who are behaving in ways that are at odds with Christian ethics?

If you're a relatively mature Christian and a self-disciplined person, travelling or living overseas by yourself may not hinder (and may even benefit) your relationship with God. You'll maintain your devotional life, seek out Christian fellowship, and resist peer group pressure. But if you think that any of these things are likely to be a challenge to you, then it may be better for you to travel with a Christian friend (or in a Christian group). Two people can keep each other accountable. As the writer of Ecclesiastes says:

> Two are better than one,
> because they have a good return for their labour:
> If either of them falls down,
> one can help the other up.
> But pity anyone who falls
> and has no-one to help them up.
> Also, if two lie down together, they will keep warm.
> But how can one keep warm alone?
> Though one may be overpowered,
> two can defend themselves.
> A cord of three strands is not quickly broken.
> (Eccl 4:9-12)

These words apply very nicely to the context of travel—not only regarding mutual spiritual support, but also regarding physical and emotional support. (Of course, I'd urge you to limit the 'lying down together' to you and your spouse or to where the two of you are lost in the wilderness in subzero temperatures and are facing hypothermia!) When the third strand in the cord is God, we have a very good situation!

If you're moving to another country to live, you might not be able to take someone with you. In this case try to find out as much as you can beforehand about Christian fellowship there. Ask your own Christian contacts or do some research online. If possible, it's always good to make contact with a pastor or someone in a Christian group before you get there. I know of one university ministry that makes a point of linking Christian students who are going overseas with believers in the country to which they're travelling, preferably before the student leaves home. For example, one student who was going to Singapore for several months was booked in to a Christian camp there before she'd even left Australia.

A staff worker from this university Christian ministry told me that she'd encouraged one student who was going abroad to give her friends several accountability questions to ask her via Skype while she was away. These questions related to how the student was going with respect to sexual purity, alcohol and church. This sort of arrangement makes a lot of sense.

It is a sad truth that travelling or living overseas with another Christian does not automatically mean that you'll do well in your spiritual life. You and your friend need to make a point of keeping each other on track. I spoke with one Christian girl who went travelling with a Christian friend.

By all accounts their general behaviour was fine, but the girl admitted that her devotional life while she was away had been pretty hopeless. While she'd given a lot of thought to their travel itinerary prior to departure, she hadn't given much thought to the priority of her quiet times. Away from the routines of home, her time with God fell in a heap. Sadly, her friend did not pick her up on this. If you'll be travelling or living overseas with another believer, make a point of discussing how you can encourage each other and perhaps keep each other accountable in key areas of your spiritual lives. Talk about this together before you leave home, as well as on a regular basis while you're away.

When it comes to travelling or living overseas with a non-Christian friend, you need to know not only yourself but also your friend. One woman I know travelled through Europe with a nonbelieving friend who, far from standing in the way of the Christian woman's quiet times, actually helped keep her accountable in this area! But it would be safe to assume that not all nonbelievers will be quite as supportive as she was. Non-Christians will naturally live in accordance with their own beliefs and ethics, and it's a question of how that is going to affect you. Some non-Christian companions will actually try to induce you to think and behave in harmful ways—"Come on, one more drink won't hurt!" Don't place yourself in a situation where you're going to spend your time overseas fighting the influence of someone who's trying to lead you astray. Know thyself, and know thy friend!

As a rule of thumb, the longer you've been a believer, the stronger your faith, and the more self-disciplined you are, the better you're likely to do spiritually while away from home. If you're a new Christian or you know that you lack self-discipline, it's probably best for you to travel with a Christian friend or group.

These three steps will help as you plan your time:

1. Organize beforehand what you'll do for your quiet times and how you'll do them.
2. Research, and perhaps organize beforehand, where you'll go to find Christian fellowship.
3. Arrange for someone—either a travel companion or a Christian back home—to regularly ask you questions that will keep you accountable in key areas such as quiet times, Christian fellowship, sexual purity, and alcohol and drugs.

If, after weighing everything up and discussing it with other believers, you think that travelling or living overseas—whether solo or with a friend—might have a negative impact on your Christian life, don't go.

But if you think (and others agree) that your trust in God is strong enough to withstand you travelling alone or moving overseas by yourself, then there are also some personality, health and gender issues to consider.

The travel writers warn (and my experience confirms) that if you're abroad by yourself, you will get lonely at times. If you're on the move, there will be periods when you won't meet up with anyone with whom you click. If you're living in one place, it will take time to settle in, integrate and develop relationships. You need to be prepared for this. It will help if you're someone who makes friends easily. It will help if you're the sort of person who is happy with your own company. If times of loneliness are likely to be a problem for you and you're planning to go solo, you may need to reconsider.

If you do decide to go it alone, I would suggest that you organize to meet up with people you know at certain points during your trip, or track down any contacts you have in places where you'll be travelling.

If you have physical or mental health struggles, it may be far wiser to travel or live overseas with another person who's both informed and sympathetic. The advice of a medical professional will help here.

Female travellers

A number of women have told me that they feel more comfortable when they're not travelling alone. For safety reasons, many choose to travel abroad with a friend, in a group, or with their spouse if they're married. Sometimes women travelling with a friend or a group decide to go solo for a short period of time and meet back up afterwards. Having said that, I do know of some women who have backpacked overseas by themselves for extended periods and found it to be a positive experience.

Of course, for those who are travelling overseas on their own to work or study or engage in some form of ministry for an extended period, it's important, as we've said, to make sure that they have a church or other Christian contacts and support structures in place when they arrive. This is true for anyone, but perhaps it's especially valuable for women (or any men, for that matter) who may be feeling vulnerable when travelling on their own.

Group tours

If you're considering whether or not to go on a group tour, the first question to address here, again, is how your decision is likely to affect your spiritual life. Will you keep up with your regular daily devotions? Do you feel you'll be able to resist any temptations placed in your way by the group? My mother once said that your IQ drops when you're in a crowd. The larger the crowd, the lower your IQ becomes.

I certainly saw evidence to support this theory on a week-long school excursion many years ago. "Hey, why don't I punch a hole in the wall of this dormitory?" Thump! "Wow, that looks cool, why don't I do it as well?" Thump! "Hmmm, nice hole. Why don't I make one here and stick my head through it?" Thump. A few blokes had a good old time and got sent home in disgrace a day or two later. Most of the guys involved would never have dreamed of damaging property on their own, but groups can make people do stupid things.

Paul writes about the potential negative influence of other people in 1 Corinthians 15: "Do not be misled: 'Bad company corrupts good character'" (v. 33). Of course, this warning needs to be balanced with what Paul says earlier in the same letter:

> I wrote to you in my letter not to associate with sexually immoral people—not at all meaning the people of this world who are immoral, or the greedy and swindlers, or idolaters. In that case you would have to leave this world. But now I am writing to you that you must not associate with anyone who claims to be a brother or sister but is sexually immoral or greedy, an idolater or slanderer, a drunkard or swindler. Do not even eat with such people. (1 Cor 5:9-11)

When we associate with nonbelievers, we are associating with people who have different beliefs and ethical standards from ours. We need to balance our desire to be salt and light (Matt 5:13-16) amongst nonbelievers with our need to prevent bad company from corrupting our character.

It can be very easy to be influenced by a group, and this applies especially to tour groups. It is certainly possible for some to effectively resist the negative influences of group behavior—remember John and Brad, the two friends we met in chapter 1, who managed to talk the entire group on a young adults' package tour of Europe out of seeing a sex show in Amsterdam. But if you don't think you can resist the peer pressure you might have to confront, it's probably wisest not to go on a group tour.

Joining a Christian tour group is always an option. While I've never participated in one of these, a friend who went on one a few years ago told me that going with a Christian organization helped her, as a 20-year-old single female traveller, to feel a certain level of comfort. Her group was welcoming, inclusive, supportive, and alcohol free, and everyone pitched in for chores. She recommends this travel option for young Christians in particular. Of course, while you might reasonably expect a good standard of behaviour in a Christian group, it's important to remember that all people are fallen people and we can't assume that any of us will always behave in a Christlike manner.

Group tours do have the advantage of saving you a lot of organizational hassle, and they give you access to people who are familiar with the countries in which you'll be travelling and who can help you with any number of things, from translation to dietary and health issues. You might also make some good friends among fellow travellers on a tour. On the downside, your travel schedule is the group's travel schedule (there's no flexibility), you may find your relationships with some other group members to be problematic, it may be hard to get any time by yourself, and it can be difficult to withstand unhelpful peer group pressure.

If you think you're up to it spiritually, then whether or not to go on a group tour—whether Christian or not—is probably a question of swings and roundabouts. Each option has its advantages and disadvantages.

The pace of travel

If you'll be travelling to different places overseas, it's important to give some thought to how much time you'll spend in each location. If you're constantly on the move, your routine will be fairly erratic, which can make having a daily devotion more of a challenge. One Christian woman said of her time abroad: "It's hard enough to read my Bible and pray at home, let alone when my routine is completely broken up and I'm seeing new things every day, and I'm tired from walking most of the time. It was just really hard."

Moving around quickly will probably mean that you're less likely to experience meaningful fellowship with other believers. But fellowship and regular daily devotions *can* be achieved on a hectic travel schedule—with discipline. The important thing is to prioritize setting aside time every day for your quiet times, as well as to visit churches in passing and stay alert to the opportunities for meeting Christians along the way. Obviously, the longer you're on the move the more you'll miss settled fellowship.

By contrast, if you live somewhere for an extended period of time—as I did in London—you'll have the opportunity to join a church, attend a Bible study group, and form some meaningful and mutually encouraging relationships.

In addition to these spiritual issues, the 'ideal' pace of travel also depends on your personality. People are full of advice about whether it's better to keep moving or to travel more slowly. Will being on the move all the time wear you out? Can you properly appreciate a place if you're just passing through? There's an old story about a couple travelling around Europe on a package tour, where the husband says to the wife, "Honey, have we seen 15 countries in 12 days or 12 countries in 15 days?" Sometimes people prefer to see lots of different things, but it does mean they're only skimming across the surface of the places they visit. The risk is that it can be hard to take it in and remember it all.

In the end, your pace of travel is a matter of personal preference, unless it's having a negative affect on your relationship with God. What appeals to some will not appeal to others. Moving quickly gives you an overview of an area or country and enables you to see some of the important sights, while stopping in one place enables you to get some rest, become a little more familiar with a place and perhaps meet a few people.

Personally, I appreciate a slightly slower pace of travel. I think I learned this by accident. Whereas travel can be fast and highly scheduled in most Western countries, moving through less developed parts of the world can force you to slow down. This is certainly the case if you attempt to travel around Sub-Saharan Africa using local transport, as I did on my first visit there. I remember one morning arriving at the bus station in Francistown, Botswana, wanting to travel to a town called Maun.

"What time does the bus leave for Maun, please?" I asked someone.

"Eleven", he told me.

"Midday", said another.

"About ten tomorrow morning", came yet another reply.

I received a different answer from every person I asked, concluding eventually that the bus *might* come sometime that day or the next. I couldn't have rushed Africa even if I'd wanted to! I quickly got used to buses without schedules, broken down trains, and long periods on roadsides waiting for lifts. Once I'd adjusted mentally, I found the experience somewhat freeing.

A few weeks later I found myself with the opposite problem. In Europe and able to move about more quickly, I was starting to feel a little worn out from all the sightseeing. When a couple of American backpackers I'd met invited me to catch the train from Florence to Pisa with them one afternoon to see its famous leaning tower, I almost said no because I was so exhausted. Being constantly on the move eventually wears you down and you can start thinking, "Oh no, not another castle!" At the end of the day it is probably better to see three European castles and appreciate them than to see 15 European castles and be bored out of your wits.

When I'm on the move I like the idea of being flexible within a basic structure. I've found it helpful to have a rough plan in mind about where I'll be going, but to remain open to changing direction or staying somewhere longer than I'd originally planned.

Travelling on the cheap or in luxury

The most important thing to consider when weighing up the level of comfort or luxury we want when we travel is whether we're being good stewards of our money. Most travel writing will have you think about what you can afford; but as believers, we want to think about being good stewards of what God has given us.

We'll think more about the spiritual issue of stewardship in chapter 7; for now we'll look at some options to consider. Most of my travel, particularly in the earlier days, was done on the cheap. On my first trip to London, as I've said, I was given free accommodation in return for playing cricket. On my nine-week backpacking adventure, I took a certain satisfaction in seeing how little I could live on—hence sleeping in a tent behind a police station (where my campsite actually turned out to be a road) to avoid paying for an expensive hotel. I lived on bread, fruit and cheese from the supermarket, only going into cafes and restaurants to order coffee and use their toilets. Others have taken budget travel to greater extremes than I did—sleeping rough regularly, and wearing the same underwear for a few days and then turning them inside-out so as to be able to wear them for a few more. Although I was budget conscious, I tried not to be so stingy that I made myself miserable. Occasionally I would pay a bit more for a travel experience or a nice meal or a more comfortable bed. When I was a bit older and no longer a student, I didn't scrape the bottom of the barrel quite as much—and by then my trips were usually much shorter. That said, I was still fairly restrained in my spending.

No doubt, my budget approach enabled me to do a little

more travelling than I would otherwise have been able to afford. Still, low-cost travel—the airfare aside—is not everyone's cup of tea. To some it may sound more like a prison sentence than an adventure. And of course there is a middle ground between budget and luxury. If you want to stay somewhere other than in youth hostels or backpacker establishments—although those places are often very pleasant—you could look at mid-range hotels and bed and breakfasts. A bit of research using something like TripAdvisor or Lonely Planet will show you what your options are so you can avoid paying for unnecessarily expensive accommodation. In recent years Airbnb, an online marketplace that allows travellers to pay to stay in private homes, has opened up other affordable alternatives.

There's also a vast range of transportation options—different classes of car, bus, train and air travel. It always pays to shop around for good flight deals, and public transport is usually the cheapest option for ground transport within cities. One fairly recent alternative to the public system is Uber, a network that links travellers with local drivers using their private cars.

As well as planning ahead to find the best options for major expenses like transportation and accommodation, other ways to keep expenses down on a trip include limiting expensive meals out, spending longer in fewer locations, thinking carefully about your purchases, and keeping a rough record of what you're spending. At the end of the day, most of the best things about travel don't cost much.

Health and safety

Health and safety are the two things I wouldn't recommend economizing on. Before each trip I always see a doctor who's up to date on what injections, pills and precautions are required for each country I am visiting. Some injections (or pills) are essential; others are optional. I usually take whatever is optional—my general rule is 'If in doubt, take the injection'. This significantly reduces the worry when I'm away. I also take an up-to-date medical kit and make sure I'm familiar with its contents. Medical professionals, travel books and websites can give good advice about what you may need in it. Similarly, before arriving in a country I try to find out whether I can drink the local water and what foods I may need to avoid.

Despite these precautions, I've still been sick at various times while I've been away. Thankfully, it has never been anything serious and each time I've been either with a friend or close to Christian contacts. One of the more challenging situations I faced was when I cut my foot quite badly. I was by myself and had to administer my own first aid—not easy, but you do what you have to do!

I take a similarly conservative approach with respect to safety. I'm all for adventure—visiting new cities, trekking in the jungle, whitewater rafting—but I never seek out danger for its own sake. As I mentioned in the last chapter, I've always tried to avoid war and situations of political unrest. Having said that, travelling in some countries is inherently riskier than travelling in others. For example, safety standards in the developing world tend to be lower than those in the West. In Kenya I was once warned before taking a shower not to touch a particular metal pipe in the cubicle. "Why not?" I asked.

"Because you might electrocute yourself", was the answer I got.

When you're visiting a new country, it's always good to find out what is and what isn't safe to do. The best option is to get the advice of trusted locals. In the absence of that, a good travel guide can help. When all else fails, use your common sense. A few times I've found myself walking around at night in areas that seemed a little dicey. When these things happen, it's best to walk quickly and look as if you know where you're going—even if you don't. Commonsense rules apply, like staying in well-lit areas where there are other people.

While travelling in the developing world involves more risk than travelling in the West, I've rarely run into difficulties. I've never been robbed or mugged. I've never been in a motor vehicle accident involving a pedestrian or other vehicle—although one vehicle in which I was a passenger foolishly tried to cross a partially washed away causeway and got stuck with two wheels suspended about a metre above the river.

And always, *always* take out travel insurance—even if you're just planning on lying on a beach for a week. Make sure the insurance covers the countries you intend to visit. You never know when you're going to have an accident, get sick, or have things stolen from you. The last thing you want is to end up in a hospital with a massive medical bill.

There may be times when you may decide, for some good reason, to accept a higher level of risk in your travels. I know people who have delivered Bibles into countries where the Scriptures are restricted, and another man who travelled into an unstable area of Africa to make a Christian video. In these cases you need to prayerfully weigh up whether you think the potential benefit is worth the risk.

We need to assess all situations that involve physical danger or a risk to our health in the light of our relationship with God and our relationships with other people. God has given us our bodies, and we need to look after them and honour God with them. As Paul writes in 1 Corinthians:

> Do you not know that your bodies are temples of the Holy Spirit, who is in you, whom you have received from God? You are not your own; you were bought at a price. Therefore honour God with your bodies. (1 Cor 6:19-20)

Travel light

It's surprising how little you need when you travel abroad. Usually I lay out all the things I think I'll need for my trip, then I pare them back to only the essential items. Then I take out a few more things before I pack. Despite all this, there are usually one or two things in my backpack or suitcase that, upon my return, I realize I haven't used. The message here is: pack light! If you're going abroad to live you might take a little more, but I still advise travelling light. If you realize you don't have something you really need, you can usually buy it somewhere.

Do some research

We've discussed the value of doing various forms of research before travelling, looking up things like churches to attend, the major religions in the countries you'll be visiting, accommodation and transportation options, and so on. There's also value in finding out what you can about the state of Christianity in the countries where you'll be.

In terms of gaining a general picture of the state of Christianity in any given country, an internet search and reading the relevant pages of Patrick Johnstone's *Operation World* will give you lots of information. In addition, reading some Christian biographies or histories should be both encouraging and informative. If you're visiting England, you might read one of the biographies about William Wilberforce; if Germany, perhaps a book about Martin Luther; if Holland, maybe Corrie ten Boom's *The Hiding Place*; if Africa, Stephen Lungu's *Out of the Black Shadows*; and if the US, perhaps Billy Graham's *Just as I Am*.

It's also helpful to learn at least a little of the language and cultural practices in the country you'll be visiting. Local people usually appreciate being greeted in their own language, and knowing a few basic phrases is useful and also shows respect. Learning how to be culturally sensitive and appropriate with regards to clothing, shopping (e.g. bartering and tipping), and in general social conduct is also important. Not only do we want to avoid being tagged 'the ugly _____ [insert your nationality here]', but this is also an application of loving our neighbours as ourselves (Mark 12:31).

Secular novels and biographies can broaden your horizons as well. It can be particularly rewarding to read a book when you're in the country where the story takes place. I found it hugely illuminating to read *A Suitable Boy*, Vikram Seth's sprawling story of life in India, while I was on the subcontinent. I also enjoyed reading Karen Blixen's *Out of Africa* while in Kenya. You can often find movies that have been set in the places where you'll be travelling, as well as travel books and documentaries. There are few places that Bill Bryson or Michael Palin have not been.

Keeping in contact

You need to keep in contact with people while you're away. Your family and friends will want to know how you're doing. Any Christian family members and friends will particularly want to know how they can pray for you and how you're doing spiritually. And, as I mentioned earlier, having someone who can keep you accountable in key areas of your Christian life will also be helpful.

Besides, it's almost always good to get news from home. When I first went travelling, we communicated by letter and telephone. With Facebook, Twitter and Skype, and the proliferation of internet cafes and smartphones, it's so much easier now. But a word of warning: try not to live on your devices. A friend told me he was recently in the common room of a backpackers' hostel and no-one was talking—everyone was staring at their screens.

While the world may be your oyster when it comes to travel, as you make your decisions, remember that you're travelling with God, in God's world, and that the most important thing by far is the 'pearl of great value' (Matt 13:45-46).

Checklist for how to travel

- Think through your 'How to travel' questions with God. Keep up with your quiet times and Christian fellowship as you work through these issues.
- Seek advice from older, wiser Christians whom you respect regarding the matters in this chapter.
- Ask how each aspect of your trip or overseas living arrangements will affect your relationship with God. Know thyself!
- When travelling or living with a friend, know thy friend. If you're planning to travel or live with a group, know thy group.
- Decide beforehand what you'll do for your quiet times and how you'll do them.
- Research and perhaps organize beforehand where you'll find Christian fellowship.
- Ask a trusted Christian friend or mentor to keep you accountable while you're away on things like quiet times, Christian fellowship, and whether you're looking for opportunities to encourage Christians and witness to non-Christians, as well as on sexual purity, alcohol and drugs.
- Consider how your plans for your trip or overseas living arrangements suit your personality. Take appropriate health and safety precautions.
- Do some research on the countries to which you'll be travelling—and especially on the state of the Christian church in those countries.
- Stay in contact with family and friends back home.
- Expect that you will be tempted to do *none* of the things suggested in this checklist. Don't let sin ruin your time abroad—or your life.

7

WHY TRAVEL?

"But seek first his kingdom and his righteousness, and all these things will be given to you as well." (Matt 6:33)

Deciding to take my first trip overseas had been such a straightforward process. I was 20 years old, a Christian, and hoping to become a professional cricketer. I thought it would be a good thing for the kingdom of God if I became a Christian sportsman. It would give me opportunities to witness to nonbelievers, as well as being an enjoyable and challenging job that involved a game I loved. A season in England would be just the thing to develop my cricketing skills and, having just finished my first university degree, the timing seemed right. I had prayed, there were good Christian reasons for the journey, my parents were supportive, and various cricketing mentors were supportive. So off I went.

Three years later, things could not have been more different. It was the sort of contrast that made chalk and cheese look similar. At 23 my cricket skills had not sufficiently developed to make 'professional cricketer' a viable career option. I had finished my university studies, but not yet started work. From a certain perspective, this period was the ideal time for an extended trip. Once I began working full-time I would be limited to the normal yearly holidays, with the next opportunity for extended overseas travel being long-service leave and, after that, retirement.

The plan floating around my brain was to buy a round-the-world air ticket and travel through southern Africa, then to England and Europe and visit friends on the way, before returning via the United States where I'd drop in on my brother in Texas. It seemed like a good idea, but I had to think long and hard about whether the trip would be a wise use of my time and money.

Should I stay or should I go? If I went, how long should I plan to be away? I prayed about it and talked with one of the ministers at my church. But in weighing up the issues, my mind lunged in opposing directions as I identified pros and cons and counter-pros and counter-cons. In retrospect I realize I was going through a fair bit of stress at the time, and my thinking was probably not at its best. In the end I settled on a nine-week trip, but the process of arriving at that decision was fraught.

Most books, blogs and articles will answer the question 'Why travel?' with a list of reasons for why you *should* travel—but I want to say something different. Regardless of what people say, you don't *have* to travel, just as you don't *have* to be involved in any other non-essential but enjoyable pursuits, such as playing football or mastering the cello. While there are many possible benefits to travelling or living abroad, there are also many good reasons for the Christian *not* to do so, or to limit their time away to some extent.

In the same way that we should *travel* with God, we should also *consider* the 'Why travel?' questions with God. As we wrestle with these issues, we need to keep praying and spending time in God's word, both on our own and with other Christians, and get on with serving God in whatever ways he has given us the opportunity. In the process God's Spirit will be maturing our faith and giving us a better understanding of his word, of his world, and of ourselves. We'll be more motivated by our new nature and less motivated by the old (Col 3:1-17). We'll be more inclined to put God's concerns first, and less inclined to hold onto our 'pet sins' and to keep certain areas of our life away from God's rule. In particular, we will want to see how Scripture guides our thinking on this topic.

The Bible describes many journeys—Abram travelling to Canaan, God's people travelling to and from Egypt, and Paul heading out on missionary journeys, to name just a few. Jesus told his disciples to "go and make disciples of all nations" (Matt 28:18-20). Obeying this command will necessitate travel at least for some, and the psalmist reassures us that wherever we go in the world, God will be there with us (Ps 139:9-10). But the Bible doesn't give us specific guidance about whether we should travel abroad for non-mission reasons, or how long our trips should be. It does, however, contain lots of wisdom that will help us to think through these decisions.

There are lots of reasons to travel abroad—for holidays, to visit relatives or friends, and for general life education, study, work and mission. Each of these purposes brings up a different set of questions and issues to consider. But whatever the circumstances, we want to make this decision in the light of God's big-picture plans for his world and for us.

Big-picture thinking

Imagine you were a fish swimming around in a bowl. You may have a very nice piece of rock and some fake seaweed to look at. Perhaps you can even see through the glass of the bowl and observe some furniture, four walls and a door. But all you know of life is this little bowl, so that is the information you use to make your decisions in life (like which bit of the fish tank you want to hang out in for the next few minutes).

Suppose that someone took you out of the bowl, put you in a clear plastic bag full of water, and walked you around the house. You would learn about kitchens and bathrooms and bedrooms. Your understanding of the world would expand exponentially. As you thought about life, you would have a much larger context to bring to bear on your musings.

Now imagine you were put in a spacecraft that blasted up into the sky, giving you views of your town, your country and then eventually affording you the chance to look back at planet Earth before speeding out into the far reaches of the galaxy. You would see a far bigger reality than you had ever previously imagined. You would understand the bigger context of which you and your fishbowl were part. With this sort of big picture, your decision-making would be transformed (unless your poor little fish brain had exploded with all this new information).

It is possible to be a very thoughtful and intelligent person and yet have a fishbowl view of life when it comes to making decisions on certain issues. When we weigh up, for example, what we're going to do on the weekend, or whether we should pursue a certain relationship, or whether we should travel or live abroad, the danger is that we can think within a very narrow context and take only a limited amount of input into account. Sometimes the input can be as narrow as 'What do I feel like doing?', or 'What do my friends think?' A Christian friend of mine named Anna recently reflected on a nine-month overseas trip she took several years ago: "I can't remember giving the decision to travel much thought, if any. In my work circles it was *the thing to do*. I also don't recall any Christian friends or leaders asking about why I was doing it."

When we think through important decisions like whether or not to go abroad, it's important to consider them within the big picture of God's plans. It's helpful to get into that spaceship, leave the earth's atmosphere, and get the larger perspective. God has graciously given us insight into his big picture, and his plans are far greater, grander and more glorious than we can imagine. Paul writes in Ephesians:

> He made known to us the mystery of his will according to his good pleasure, which he purposed in Christ, to be put into effect when the times reach their fulfillment —to bring unity to all things in heaven and on earth under Christ. (Eph 1:9-10)

God's big-picture plan for his creation is to bring all things under Christ—everyone and everything, everywhere. What's more, God chooses to use us in his purposes. What a privilege! As God's people, then, we need to do all our thinking, including our thinking about travelling and living abroad, with an awareness of this big picture.

As Christians who have repented and trusted in Jesus as

our Lord and Saviour, we are the recipients of so many benefits that God in his kindness showers upon us. He has saved us from the judgement we deserve; forgiven us; adopted us into his family; and given us the Holy Spirit, eternal life, and purpose, power and wisdom for this earthly life. He has also given us life, health (well, at least enough health to read this book), family, relationships, church, time, money and talents. Of course, we will also face suffering and persecution in this life—and these can be very severe—but, as believers, we know that God is working for our good in everything (Rom 8:28-30), and that nothing can separate us from the love of God (Rom 8:38-39). God has given us everything we need for a godly life (2 Pet 1:3), and every spiritual blessing in Christ (Eph 1:3). How could we not want to serve a God who has done all this for us?

Of course, the repentance we expressed when we became Christians means that we have resolved to follow Jesus, to put him first in our lives. He is our captain, our king; the person we want to honour in all our decisions. It's no longer a case of 'What do I want?' but, rather, 'What would Jesus want?' Our lives are not our own—they're his.

In some ways it should not be a problem for us to trust Jesus with our decisions, given that we have put our lives into the hands of someone who is so powerful, so wise, and who loves us so much. Still, sadly it can often be quite a challenge to relinquish the reins. We are sometimes foolishly tempted to think that God is a killjoy, or that we know better than he does. On this side of heaven, our lives are something of a battle between our new nature, which is controlled by the Spirit and desires the things of God, and our old nature—the sinful nature (or 'flesh') that has no interest in God's concerns. Paul writes in Galatians 5:

> So I say, walk by the Spirit, and you will not gratify the desires of the flesh. For the flesh desires what is contrary to the Spirit, and the Spirit what is contrary to the flesh. They are in conflict with each other, so that you are not to do whatever you want. (vv. 16-17)

Our new nature will be keen to see how God would have us think about travelling or living abroad; our old nature will resist what God thinks. What a tragedy it would be to let our old nature control our thinking on this issue!

So how do we know what God want us to do in this life? Well, Jesus teaches that all of the Old Testament commands are based on two underlying principles: loving God and loving our neighbour. When asked by an expert in the Old Testament law about which was the greatest commandment, Jesus replied:

> "'Love the Lord your God with all your heart and with all your soul and with all your mind.' This is the first and greatest commandment. And the second is like it: 'Love your neighbour as yourself'. All the Law and the Prophets hang on these two commandments." (Matt 22:37-40)

Given God's unchanging character, these same two principles of loving God and loving our neighbour also underlie the teaching of the New Testament (e.g. John 14:15; Rom 13:8). If everyone loved God and loved their neighbour we'd all find ourselves living within a network of mutual-love relationships. What a great world that would be! It would be the sort of world that God desires—it would be the kingdom of God.

Christian ethicist Michael Hill conceives of the Christian life as seeking to promote "mutual love relationships" between God and people, and between people and people.[23] Of course, what love looks like will vary from situation to situation. The way a person loves their parents differs from the way in which they love their spouse, which differs from the way they love their children, their friends, their brothers and sisters at church, other road users, people in other countries, and future generations. But in all our various relationships, as we obey Jesus and promote mutual love relationships, we'll devote ourselves to four relational goals:

- growing in our relationship with God
- helping others get into, and grow in, relationship with God
- growing in our relationships with others
- helping others get into, and grow in, relationships with others.

These goals help us to see more clearly the importance of Bible reading, prayer, encouraging other believers, evangelism, discipleship, helping those in need, working for reconciliation, and other acts of love and mercy. As we prayerfully participate in these things, we fulfil our purpose in life and God's kingdom grows. We are part of something big.

23 Michael Hill argues that the unifying theme behind all the ethical teaching of the Bible can be summarized in the following "mutual love ethic (ML)": "ML = An action or trait of character is right if and only if it promotes (creates or maintains) mutual love relationships between (a) God and humans, and, (b) humans and humans" (Michael Hill, *The How and Why of Love: An Introduction to Evangelical Ethics*, Matthias Media, Sydney, 2002, p. 131).

There's an old story told of two medieval stonecutters who were interviewed as they worked at the site of a new cathedral. The first was asked, "What do you do?"

"I chip stones all day", he replied.

When the second was asked the same question, he proudly proclaimed, "I'm building a great cathedral". As Christians, we're involved in building something far greater than a great cathedral. We are part of something eternal!

When we think through the decisions in our lives—whether or not they relate to travelling abroad—we want to use big-picture thinking. We want our new nature, which desires the things of God, to guide our minds. And we want to think through what kind of impact our plans will have on those four relational goals set out above.

In the light of all that, then, how can we follow Jesus better as we make decisions in the area of travel? I would suggest that it is good to travel if:

Step 1: we consider that we're travelling for good, godly reasons
Step 2: we consider the trip to be good stewardship of the time and money God has given to us
Step 3: we've thoughtfully considered the trip's potential impact on key relationships.

We need to think about each of these aspects, ideally with the help of a mature Christian believer. Just because there may be some good reasons to travel, this does not mean that we *should* travel. There might be some stewardship or relationship issues that tip the scales in favour of staying at home, travelling at another time, or considering a shorter time away.

Let's now consider each of these steps in turn.

Step 1: Consider our reasons for travelling

People describe their trips overseas in lots of different ways. They may say they're going on a holiday, an adventure, a quest or a pilgrimage. They may talk about taking a gap year, visiting relatives or friends, doing a short-term mission, or going overseas to work or to study. However it is expressed, I think the common reasons for travelling to another country can be boiled down to the following:

i. for leisure
ii. to deepen or maintain particular relationships
iii. for education
iv. for work
v. to do ministry
vi. because everyone else is doing it
vii. to find the meaning of life
viii. to escape life's difficulties
ix. to feel superior.

I'd say that the first five reasons are good reasons to travel, while the final four are not. It's also true, of course, that someone might take a trip for a combination of different reasons.

i. Leisure

Many people travel purely for leisure, sometimes within their own country and sometimes abroad. In order to work out whether or not this is a good reason for travelling, we need to think a little about what 'leisure' is.

Leisure is a God-given gift to be enjoyed. It might be defined as "that part of a person's life that is not devoted to earning money, performing necessary duties (in home, society, church, and so on), and sleeping".[24] We can think about leisure in terms of rest, recreation, stimulation or adventure. What someone actually considers to be leisure will vary from person to person—it could be anything from reading to bushwalking, playing guitar or throwing a javelin.

While the Christian church has given the topic of 'work' a lot of thought, the topic of 'leisure' has been somewhat neglected. Leland Ryken notes that "The church has usually either condemned leisure as worldly and unworthy of a spiritually minded person, or has imitated the practices of secular society".[25] We don't want to fall into either trap.

A detailed Christian account of leisure is beyond the scope of this book, but we can see in the Scriptures that:

- God worked to create the world and then he rested (Genesis 1-2; Exod 31:17)
- God instituted a Sabbath day in the Old Testament on which people were not to work (Exod 20:8-11)
- Jesus said, "The Sabbath was made for man, not man for the Sabbath" (Mark 2:27)
- after a time of busy ministry, Jesus told his disciples, "Come with me by yourselves to a quiet place and get some rest" (Mark 6:31)
- Jesus frequently attended dinner parties and social gatherings (e.g. Luke 10:38-42, 19:1-10; John 2:1-11)

24 PD Toon, 'Leisure', in RK Harrison (ed.), *The Encyclopedia of Biblical Ethics*, Testament, New York, 2003, p. 229.
25 L Ryken, 'Leisure', in David J Atkinson, David F Field, Arthur Holms and Oliver O'Donovan (eds), *New Dictionary of Christian Ethics and Pastoral Theology*, IVP, Leicester, 1995, p. 547.

- the Bible describes the new Jerusalem as a place where boys and girls will play in the streets (Zech 8:5).

The Bible clearly presents leisure as a good thing but, like all things in this fallen world, sinful people can and do misuse it (and that includes Christians, since we still sin). For example, we do not want to let leisure drift into idleness (2 Thess 3:6), or let it become an idol, or allow it to become an opportunity for immorality. Rather, leisure is something we want to enjoy in a godly way. God is pro-rest and pro-recreation. Paul writes that people should "put their hope in God, who richly provides us with everything for our enjoyment" (1 Tim 6:17), and that "everything God created is good, and nothing is to be rejected if it is received with thanksgiving" (1 Tim 4:4).

If we're travelling primarily for leisure, we need to consider the trip in terms of whether it's a wise use of our money and time and also in the light of how it will impact our relationships. We will discuss these matters shortly, but for now we can simply note that leisure is a good, God-given gift, and that travelling can be a good way to use our leisure time.

ii. Relationships

As we saw above in those four relational goals, relationships are central to God's purposes for the world. The creation, strengthening and restoration of relationships are all good reasons to travel. I've already mentioned some of my visits to various family members and friends, including my brother in the United States and a relative in England, as well as the friend in Germany whose wedding I attended. Over the years I've also formed new and significant relationships on my travels, such as with my ASIF and cricket friends in London and with various African believers I've met on my lecturing visits.

iii. Education

Travel for the sake of education usually takes one of two forms: travel for the purposes of study at an overseas institution, and travel for what might be termed 'general life education'. My eldest brother, for example, moved from Australia to Texas to do his doctorate in a particular area of science. Some courses that you might do in your home country will involve an overseas component for a few weeks, a term, or longer. Formal study overseas can take many other forms as well. Professionals attend international conferences in their fields, for example, and many Christians go on study tours of the Holy Land.

By 'general life education', I mean the things a person can learn from visiting new places, seeing new things, meeting new people, and putting themselves in new situations. In the same way that field trips benefit our learning at school, international travel can enrich our education as adults.

Throughout the Bible, God encourages us to continue learning. Our most important topic of study, of course, is God—and we learn about who he is, what he's done and how we're to follow him by reading his word. But God also encourages us to learn more about him and his world through the wonders of his creation—for example, from the majesty of the heavens (Ps 8:3-4), the untiring industry of creatures like the ant (Prov 6:6-8) and the wise beauty of the seasons (Mark 13:28-29).

We will be assisted in this process if we live, study or travel overseas with the right eyewear. I refer here not to the latest in fashion sunglasses, but to Calvin's spectacles. The famous Reformer John Calvin compared Scripture to a pair of spectacles that enables us to clearly see and properly interpret the world about us. If we view what we see and experience in the light of God's word, travel will be a great education. Some say that 'travel broadens the mind', but I think it would be better to say that travel *can* broaden the mind—if we view our experiences through the lens of Scripture.

We need to remember, however, that many of the things you can learn from observing the world while travelling overseas can also be learned from observing the world in a similar way at home. You don't *need* to live or travel abroad to appreciate the glory of God's creation or the devastating impact of sin in this fallen world. In fact, in the centuries before overseas travel became affordable for the masses, people were still appreciating creation and comprehending the devastation caused by sin. If you are abroad, however, you will have different opportunities to learn and grow in wisdom. Seeing poverty first hand, or experiencing Christian fellowship in a different culture, for example, can impress particular truths upon you in new ways.

We also sometimes learn unexpected things while we're away from home. For me, it was in the area of my personal development. Making my own way in a foreign country when I was 20 years old meant that I developed a few life skills and grew in self-confidence more quickly than I would have at home. I learned about washing, cleaning and cooking; about organizing my time; and about meeting and getting along with people from different cultures. I came back from that trip a far more mature person.

My time away also greatly enhanced my understanding of and appreciation for Australia. We learn a lot by having a frame of reference for comparison. I learned new things about my family, my church and my city by comparing them to the families, churches and cities I encountered in my travels. Being overseas increased my appreciation for what I had at home. I also learned, in a new and deeper way, that Sydney is *not* the world.

iv. Work

People often go abroad for work-related reasons as well. While some intentionally seek a job or work transfer oversees, sometimes employers will recommend a work trip overseas or an international transfer. (I would categorize a working holiday, where a person picks up jobs while travelling predominantly to fund a longer time away, as a holiday taken mainly for the purpose of leisure.)

Work is part of God's plan for humanity (e.g. Gen 2:15; 1 Thess 4:11-12) and may sometimes involve travel, especially in this day and age when travel has become much more affordable. Depending on the circumstances, this can be a good reason to go abroad. Of course, our motives and life context will be relevant here. Work, I believe appropriately and for good reason, has taken me to India and Africa. As I've said, I've also taken opportunities to extend time abroad for work by adding a few days or weeks of travel for leisure, relationships or general life education.

v. Ministry

In listing 'ministry' as a reason for going abroad, I am not primarily thinking of missionaries who travel to engage in full-time ministry—that is a larger question for other books. Rather, I am thinking about other sorts of mission-related trips. These may be short-term missions or ministry trips lasting anything from a week to a few months or longer. They might be organized by theological colleges, churches, schools or para-church organizations, or by individuals themselves. While some question the benefits of short-term missions (and again, entering into this discussion is beyond the scope of this book), I would argue that in many cases such trips can be of great benefit to both the people doing the mission and the people being served by the mission. Many a struggling missionary has been refreshed and comforted by a visit from friends and likeminded believers. If a mission trip is genuinely helpful, it is a good reason for travelling.

There are other possibilities for ministry-related travel, too. A friend of mine involved in university Christian ministry says to students with an interest in distant lands, "Don't just go overseas—live overseas!" If you're a keen Christian, why not consider working in a foreign country for a few years? Whether you are a teacher, a nurse, an engineer, or something else—the main thing is to live, work, encourage other Christians, and witness to nonbelievers there. If you have some ability in a particular language or an affinity for people from a certain region, that may help narrow the field where you have multiple options. My friend recommends finding a church or missionary who could use some assistance, or identifying an area of the world that could do with a Christian presence. Some of my friend's former students have gone to work in Indonesia and New Zealand for this very reason. And, of course, full-time missionary work is also an option to consider.

These are all good reasons to consider travelling; now for some poor reasons.

vi. Everyone else is

Overseas travel among young people is becoming increasingly common. The Australian Government's Smart Traveller website notes that "Backpacking is considered by many Australians as a rite-of-passage into the world". And, as I mentioned earlier, for my friend Anna and her workmates, travelling was "the thing to do". In some subcultures, going abroad in the decade or so after finishing high school is now almost the norm.

But going overseas simply because everyone else is doing it is a very poor reason to leave home. It reveals a shallow level of thought and suggests that we are more influenced by other people than by God. As Christians, we'll always find ourselves making different life choices from those around us. When it comes to whether, why and how we travel, we want to be cultural thermostats, not thermometers; we want to regulate the temperature of our surroundings and not simply reflect it. God and his word are our ultimate guides—not other people.

vii. Meaning of life

Some people embark very deliberately on a quest overseas to find the meaning of life. In recent decades it has become popular for Westerners to go to the East in search of a guru or some spiritual insight into life. A particularly well-known and influential example of this is The Beatles' visit in the late 1960s to the ashram of Maharishi Mahesh Yogi in India, where they explored the world of Transcendental Meditation. Christians know that the meaning of life is found in Christ, and we know that Christ can be encountered anywhere—at home or overseas. Most Christians aren't likely to consciously go travelling to find the meaning of life.

However, a 'meaning of life' motivation *can* seep into the minds of believers at a more insidious level. While there are many potential benefits to travelling, it is possible for travel itself to become our 'meaning of life'. Travel can turn into an idol, an obsession. It can start to occupy our thoughts and emotions to such an extent that we no longer appreciate normal life. Home becomes mundane. Ministry seems a little boring. Our work only serves to help us save enough money for our next trip. We can begin to channel all of our thoughts and energies in this direction. An unhelpful fixation on travel can be a very real danger for some people.

Paul's teaching in 1 Timothy is helpful here: "But godliness with contentment is great gain" (1 Tim 6:6). If you become aware of an unhealthy fixation on travel in your life then can I encourage you to repent, work on your relationship with God, and seek the counsel of a Christian you respect.

viii. Escape

All over the world there are travellers and expats who appear to be running away from something. They're abroad to avoid a relationship, or work, or their former lifestyle. But escape is a bad reason to go overseas. It's always best to address and deal with problems, and as Christians we will seek to do this in a godly way. Sometimes we might take a holiday or move away as part of a wise, considered response to a difficult situation, but we shouldn't use travel as a means of avoidance. Again, if this is a problem for you, it's important to repent, work on your relationship with God, and seek godly counsel.

ix. To feel superior

Perhaps you have been to a party or a dinner where someone has gone on and on about their recent trip overseas—how great it was, how they went to this place and that, how they went off the beaten track, how they gained so many new insights and really got to know the locals. And—by implication—what a sad, narrow, commercial, unenlightened, boring bunch the rest of you are in comparison, and how fortunate you are to be able to sit at their feet and receive the benefit of their wisdom.

Travel can certainly refresh and educate, but in actual fact no-one is a better person simply by virtue of having travelled or lived abroad. Travelling does not place us on a higher social pedestal or Christian plane. If you've seen Christian ministry operating in, say, the poorer areas of Africa, you may return home with insights on Christian service, or on materialism in the West. However, if you have learned anything, you'll want to use that knowledge to serve others, not to place yourself above them. This seems to be the idea Paul is getting at when he writes, "knowledge puffs up while love builds up" (1 Cor 8:1). Travelling to help us feel superior to others, or to bolster our self-esteem, is a very bad reason to travel.

We have identified some good and bad reasons to travel or live overseas. If we conclude that our reasons for going abroad are good ones, we then move on to the second step in our three-step assessment process.

Step 2: Consider our stewardship of what God has given us

A steward is someone who manages another person's property. Stewards are responsible for looking after the property, but they don't own it. 'Stewardship' describes humanity's relationship to God's creation. Genesis 2:15 explains that God placed human beings in his world "to work it and take care of it". We are stewards charged with the task of looking after everything that God has made.

As Christians we also realize that everything good is a gift from God. James 1 says, "Every good and perfect gift is from above, coming down from the Father of the heavenly lights, who does not change like shifting shadows" (v. 17). God has given us the gospel, the natural world, our relationships, and the society in which we live, as well as personal resources such as time, money and talents. As stewards of all these things, we're answerable to God for how we use them (e.g. Matt 25:14-30).

Particularly relevant for questions relating to travelling or living overseas is our stewardship of the time and money that God has given us. Is it wise to spend our time and money on going abroad? If we conclude that in our particular circumstances it is wise, then for how long should we go and how much should we spend? Over the years I've tried to be a good steward of time and money in all areas of my life. What constitutes good stewardship has often seemed fairly clear to me, but there have been times when the way forward was a little hazier (e.g. just before my second trip overseas).

There is no simple, sure-fire formula for good stewardship. However, if we're walking closely with God, meditating on his word, and seeking the counsel of wise Christians, we'll be in a much better position to answer the following questions with a fair degree of wisdom: Does our proposed use of time and money reflect God's priorities for our lives? How might we assess (or reassess) our plans in the light of God's big-picture plans for his creation?

Time

Is it a wise use of our time to travel or live abroad? And, if so, how much of our life should we give to it? Our motivations for travel are particularly relevant here. We know that leisure, relationships, education, work and ministry are all good reasons that may prompt a person to leave home (step 1). However, when we consider these motivations in the light of Scripture, it's clear that it is wiser to contemplate spending more time away for some reasons than for others. To state the obvious, it may be very wise to devote a lifetime to overseas mission, but it would be very unwise to devote a lifetime to international leisure travel.

The Bible does give some guidelines to those planning to travel for leisure—for example, we have already noted that leisure is good but being idle is bad (2 Thess 3:6). But the Scriptures do not identify the exact point at which leisure time starts to drift into idleness. All mature Christians would rightly endorse times of leisure, and leisure may very well involve travel. All mature Christians would rightly question excessive leisure travel, since believers need to devote time to things like work and regular ministry (e.g. Eph 4:28; 1 Pet 4:10). As to how many weeks or months of leisure travel is too much—I cannot tell you.

Personally, I'm of the view that time spent overseas for reasons of work, formal study and ministry might wisely extend for a number of years, whereas a trip taken purely for leisure will probably last no more than a few weeks or months. If a leisure trip also involved some general life education, ministry and/or relational opportunities (such as visiting family or friends), it might last a little longer without spiraling into idleness. But this is my personal opinion, and you need to work this question out for yourself.

Most people who are working or studying are limited to a set amount of holiday time each year. Depending on your circumstances, it might be appropriate to use some or all of this time for the purposes of going overseas. But remember that you don't *need* to use all the time you have available for international travel—you may decide to use some of your holiday time to volunteer for a Christian ministry such as a Christian camp or a children's holiday ministry at your church.

People often have the opportunity to travel for a longer period between study and work. For example, many people finishing high school have the opportunity to take a gap year, and many people finishing university take a long trip before starting work. Other opportunities for longer travel include long-service leave, time between jobs, and during retirement. But again, just because such travel is possible doesn't mean that we should do it, or that we should go for as long as we could. There are other aspects to consider.

Money

What is an appropriate amount to spend on travelling or living overseas? Again, the Bible gives some guidelines but doesn't lay down specific rules. The Scriptures tell us that we should use our money to look after ourselves (1 Thess 4:11-12), our family (1 Tim 5:8), those in Christian ministry (1 Tim 5:17-18), and the needy (Eph 4:28).

In my view, deciding on an appropriate amount of money to spend on going abroad depends significantly on our reasons for travel, how much money we have, and what other financial responsibilities we have. Different people will work through the issues differently. As with our stewardship of time, my personal view is that we might wisely spend more money going and living overseas for reasons of work, formal study and ministry than we would on a trip undertaken purely for leisure. Again, if a leisure trip also involved some general life education and/or relational opportunities (such as visiting family or friends), we might wisely spend a little more.

We can get into murky waters when we start to consider how our travel fits into the overall picture of our financial responsibilities. The capacity here for sinful self-delusion can be huge. Paul warns that "the love of money is a root of all kinds of evil" (1 Tim 6:10). We are often quick to spend money on ourselves and on our families, but not on others. One Christian man I know poses the question: Is it right to spend more money on leisure travel than I give to church or mission? It's a question worth asking. Unfortunately, Christians can often lack generosity towards churches and other Christian organizations. Many churches struggle to meet their yearly budgets. It's a rare church building program that raises the required money without going through some grief. And most mission and charity organizations have to work very hard to raise even the most basic level of funding.

While I do not want to present myself as a perfect example, in working out my budget over the years my practice has been to first set aside a certain percentage of the money I earn for Christian ministry. I also make sure that I can look after my family and myself. I then try to support various charities and people in need. It is only after this that I have what might be termed 'disposable income'. I've spent some of this on travel for leisure/general life education/relationships. I hope I'm not deluding myself, but over the years I don't believe that my travelling has had an impact on the percentage of money I've given to Christian ministry. It *has* probably resulted in my buying a slightly smaller house, driving a less expensive car, and spending less money on other leisure pursuits.

Step 3: Consider the impact of travel on our relationships

It should be clear by now that travelling and living overseas can be beneficial for certain relationships, especially with family and friends who live abroad. But travel also has an impact on key relationships back home—with our family, our friends and our church. Generally speaking, it could be said that the longer the trip, the greater the potential impact on these relationships.

Our relationships with family

If you're not married, your primary family relationships will probably be with your parents, and perhaps also with your siblings and grandparents. The usual worries aside, family members will generally be comfortable with you going abroad for a few weeks or months if they think you're responsible, your reasons for travelling are worthwhile, and you're not going to do anything unnecessarily dangerous. But if there's serious illness in the family, or if someone is in some way dependent upon you, your considerations will be different—particularly if you're planning an extended time abroad for study, work or short-term ministry. These are factors you would need to think about.

If you're married, you might go overseas with your spouse and children (if you have children). In some cases, however, this is neither possible nor practical. As a husband and father, I much prefer travelling with my family than on my own. I've been on a number of two-week lecturing trips to Africa since I've been married, however, and it hasn't been practical to take my family with me. Before I was married, I often added a holiday onto the end of my teaching stints—anything from a week to a month or so. Now that I have a family back home I'm much keener to return quickly. Sometimes I might visit a wildlife park for two or three days after my teaching responsibilities are finished, but I keep it to that.

Our relationships with friends

Again, friends will usually be encouraging about the idea of you travelling for a few weeks or months. Sometimes, however, there are particularly close relationships to which you will need to give special consideration—for example, if you have a boyfriend or girlfriend. While they will no doubt miss you if you're away for a couple of weeks, it's another thing to tell them that you're thinking of going away for six months or more. These kinds of travel plans would clearly raise questions about how the two of you view your relationship. If the reason for travel is predominantly leisure, plans to be away for that long may suggest a certain lack of commitment to the relationship. If the reason for travel is something more 'essential' like, for example, work or study, the two of you may consider that the trip is important and worth the sacrifice. Communication will be important for maintaining your relationship.

Our relationship with church

This is an important consideration and one that can be easily overlooked. Some of the most significant things we do in life are our ministries at church. If you're a Sunday School teacher, for example, your absence will require someone else to teach your classes. This may place a strain on other leaders at the church. Your absence will also have an impact on your relationship with the children you teach. While an absence of a few weeks will often be fairly easy to deal with, an absence of half a year is more invasive. It is not necessarily a reason not to go overseas for this period of time, but it is certainly a very important aspect to consider.

If you do decide to go away and it will affect your ministry in some way, make sure you give your ministry leaders as much notice as possible.

What if I'm already travelling?

It may be that you are reading this book while you're already living or travelling overseas. If it has caused you to think a little more deeply about your reasons for what you're doing and you have been reaffirmed about the value of your time away, that's great! Thank God and continue to make the most of this opportunity for his kingdom. Use this time to grow in your relationship with God and in your understanding of God's world. And as you grow in your relationships with others, make the most of opportunities to help them get into relationship with God and grow in him.

If, on the other hand, you're now questioning the value of your time away, I would urge you to do a few things: work on your relationship with God and seek out Christian fellowship; confess to God any sins of which you've become aware; live a godly life where you are now; prayerfully consider the future; and seek counsel from wise Christians. You might decide to remain abroad, but now with a godlier mindset and motives. Great! You'll be able to make the most of the rest of your trip for the kingdom of God. You might instead, after prayer and consideration, decide to cut your trip short and return home.

In any case, remember that if you have made mistakes and you have repented, God is a gracious and forgiving God. We all make mistakes, and there's no sin so great that it's beyond the capacity of Jesus' death on the cross to forgive. You can also take comfort in knowing that God can redeem our mistakes and use them for good.

If you do decide to cut your trip short, try not to lose sight of the positives in your journey so far, even if they are linked in with a whole lot of disobedience and thoughtlessness.

Finally, I would add: do not be too hard on yourself. Everything we do as Christians is done with a mixture of motives. The aim is to try to maximize the godly motives and minimize the ungodly ones.

A combination trip

Let's say that, having wisely considered steps 1, 2 and 3, you find yourself with the opportunity to spend some extended time away—perhaps between study and work. It may be great to plan some leisure travel, but why not consider combining it with some other travel goals? I know of one young woman who spent some time between school and university helping at an orphanage in Indonesia and another who, when visiting a missionary family, was able to care for their children so the parents could go out together in the evening. There are countless opportunities, as we've seen, for connecting with people and serving God and others around the world.

I also know a minister who took his teenage son along on a short-term lecturing trip to Africa a few years ago. He wanted to provide his son with some general life education, and they also visited a missionary and enjoyed a short holiday together. The minister recently told me:

> As I look back on this time in my son's life I see how valuable it really was. He continues to have a compassionate concern for Christians in tough places and for leadership development. He intends to go to theological college after he has spent a few years in the secular workforce.

My travels today

As I write, my wife and I have a nine-year-old son and an eight-year-old daughter. There's very little time for backpacking these days, and holidays are more family affairs—usually beachside (or 'beachnear') cabins or simple road trips. But that's okay. I *love* our holidays, although they may not sound that exciting to the outsider. There are seasons in our lives and I'm very grateful to God for where I am now. As I've said, overseas travel is by no means a necessity.

But my involvement with the program that provides theological education to untrained African leaders has also enabled me to visit Africa eight times over the past ten years. While I've gone out of a desire to help equip the African church, I've also learned a lot *from* the African church, met some wonderful African Christians, made some good friends, and gained some great insights into African life. And in my short add-on holidays before or after lecturing I've sometimes found myself once again rubbing shoulders with backpackers. And when they ask me what I'm doing in Africa, interesting discussions sometimes follow!

Checklist for deciding whether or not to travel

- Think through the 'Why travel' questions with God. Keep up with your quiet times and Christian fellowship as you work through these questions.
- Seek advice from older, wiser Christians you respect regarding the matters in this chapter.
- Try to keep God's big-picture concerns and relationship priorities in mind as you consider going abroad.

- Work through the three-step process:

  Step 1: Do you think you're travelling for good, godly reasons, or are you more influenced by worldly reasons?

  Step 2: Do you think that your travel plans constitute good stewardship of the time and money God has given you?

  Step 3: Have you considered the impact of your travel plans on key relationships?

- Expect that you will be tempted to do *none* of the things suggested in this checklist. Don't let sin ruin your time abroad—or your life.

CONCLUSION

And whatever you do, whether in word or deed, do it all in the name of the Lord Jesus, giving thanks to God the Father through him. (Col 3:17)

Going home

Five months and innumerable cups of tea later, I was back on a British Airways flight returning to Sydney—a different person. Not only had I turned 21, but my Christian life had really pushed on as well. Being away from home and sometimes out of my comfort zone had made me more consciously reliant on God. Long periods of time on my own had given me plenty of time to study the Bible, pray and reflect. I'd read Christian books, listened to Christian music, and talked with other believers. I'd joined a church my minister had recommended and become part of its international fellowship group.

I'd also made good friends at the cricket club. I'd put my Christian faith on the table early on, provoking everything from bemusement to genuine interest, and people had noticed that my behaviour was different. In between cricket games and Christian meetings, I'd had the opportunity to explore England, Scotland and Wales. I'd also ventured onto the Continent and up into Scandinavia to see things that had once only existed for me on the pages of school projects.

Living overseas, like living at home, had its ups and downs. On some days I felt closer to God than on others. I'd taken some opportunities to talk about my faith and missed others. I'd had good and bad days on the cricket field. I'd met many people with whom I got on, and some with whom I didn't. At times I was so happy I could cry, at other times I was frustrated, and at still other times I felt sad.

But that was all recent history. As I flew over Europe I flicked through my photographs, wrote in my diary and felt an overwhelming sense of gratitude to God. Before I knew it, I'd landed in Sydney and was reunited with my parents and friends. It felt as if I'd only just left.

Back home

Travel writing is full of advice about what *not* to do when you return home from overseas. Chief among these tips is the exhortation to *not* bore people with your travel stories. Our transnational tales, as significant as they may be to us, are far less captivating for others. Some family and friends will be interested in hearing a bit about our experiences. They may even be happy to sit down and look at photos for half an hour. But, your mother aside (and she's probably only being encouraging), no-one will be fascinated by your detailed musings on the various cloud formations depicted in the 102 photographs you took out of the window during the flight between Amsterdam and New York.

As we discussed in the last chapter, try to avoid the temptation to arrogantly think that you've been transformed while everyone at home has remained the same. God willing, you will have changed—but so have those at home, who have probably been sticking at the important work of continuing their studies, working, looking after their families, and persevering in their ministries.

So what *do* you have to share with others when you return? Well, if you have a deeper relationship with God, this will inform everything you do to the benefit of others. It will impact the way you relate to people and the way you serve in ministry. You may also have new friendships to maintain with people you met while you were away. These relationships provide opportunities for ongoing encouragement, witness and prayer. And, sure, hopefully you will have a few stories to pull out (in moderation) at parties and dinners over the following months.

Make sure you thank God for the opportunities he's given you, and be sure to also thank those who supported you—either financially or in prayer—while you were away. Make sure you get back into church life and Christian service. Ask that God would use you and the things he's taught you to further the work of his kingdom. You might decide to pray for and financially support Christians and Christian ministries in the countries in which you've lived or visited. You might even find, as I have, that God uses aspects of your travels further down the track for his purposes.

Travelling and living overseas can be a real spiritual plus or minus. I know of two young men, both youth leaders, who left Australia to study in the US. Both were encouraged to join a church while abroad, and while they were away their home church pastors and friends prayed for them and kept in contact. Over in the States one of them joined a university Christian group, got involved with evangelistic missions, and came back to Australia full of spiritual zeal. The other joined a church, but started dating a nonbeliever. His overseas friends did not pull him up on this, and the young man kept his Australian Christian friends in the dark about what was going on. In the end, he pulled away from the church and no longer lives as a follower of Jesus.

The person who told me this story suggested that the important difference between the two leaders was that the first went away with not only a determination to be godly, but also a plan of how to do so; and he surrounded himself with people who kept him accountable.

Travel can help you to think and act 'internationally' as a believer. You don't need to go overseas to be a global Christian, but it would be a tragedy if you went overseas and didn't come back as one.

If you're considering going abroad, my prayer is that you'll weigh up all the different aspects of this decision with prayerful godly wisdom. If you're soon to go abroad, my prayer is that you will do what is needed so that you go away spiritually prepared. If you're currently abroad, my prayer is that you will travel with God through God's fallen world with a view to encouraging believers and pointing everyone else towards Christ. In this way, for the Christian abroad, the far-flung corners of our planet will be mission fields, not mine-fields. And remember that whatever you decide and wherever you find yourself, following Jesus is the ultimate trip.

ACKNOWLEDGEMENTS

This book could never have been completed without the generous support and assistance of many people.

I would particularly like to thank Anglican Churches Springwood for allowing me time off to do much of the writing; Simon Pillar for his encouragement and very practical support; Emma Thornett, Ian Carmichael, and the rest of the team at Matthias Media, who have been an absolute pleasure to work with; and Tara Smith and Kerrie Thomas for their assistance in the early stages of the editing process.

I am also indebted to the travellers, parents and ministers I consulted when writing this book, who provided me with input for the text and feedback on it—they know who they are!

Three cheers also to Wikipedia—a wonderfully helpful resource.

I am especially thankful for the support of my family—my two children, Bill and Charlotte (one of whom would have preferred that I was writing a children's book), and most especially for my wife, Shareen, who has been an unending source of encouragement both in this endeavour as well as in the rest of my life!

Finally and most of all, I am grateful, in more ways that I can express, to God—the creator of this world and those who travel it. If any aspect of this book is of any help to anyone, to God be the glory!

APPENDIX: TWO WAYS TO LIVE

This is an abbreviated form of the *Two Ways to Live* gospel presentation. For the full presentation, see **www.twowaystolive.com** or the printed version available from Matthias Media: *Two Ways to Live: The choice we all face*. Scripture quotations in this appendix are from the 1984 translation of the NIV.

The message at the heart of Christianity is really quite simple—simple enough to be outlined in a few pages. It is a message from the Bible about God and his son, Jesus. It is about life and death, and the choice that we all face.

And it all starts with a loving creator God…

1. God is the loving ruler of the world. He made the world. He made us rulers of the world under him.

   You are worthy, our Lord and God, to receive glory and honour and power, for you created all things, and by your will they were created and have their being. (Revelation chapter 4, verse 11)

   But is that the way it is now?

2. We all reject the ruler—God—by trying to run life our own way without him. But we fail to rule ourselves or society or the world.

   There is no-one righteous, not even one; there is no-one who understands, no-one who seeks God. All have turned away. (Romans chapter 3, verses 10-12)

   What will God do about this rebellion?

3. God won't let us rebel forever. God's punishment for rebellion is death and judgement.

   Man is destined to die once, and after that to face judgement. (Hebrews chapter 9, verse 27)

   God's justice sounds hard. But...

4. Because of his love, God sent his Son into the world: the man Jesus Christ. Jesus always lived under God's rule. Yet by dying in our place he took our punishment and brought forgiveness.

   Christ died for sins once for all, the righteous for the unrighteous, to bring you to God. (1 Peter chapter 3, verse 18)

   But that's not all...

5. God raised Jesus to life again as the ruler of the world. Jesus has conquered death, now gives new life, and will return to judge.

   In his great mercy he has given us new birth into a living hope through the resurrection of Jesus Christ from the dead. (1 Peter chapter 1, verse 3)

   Well, where does that leave us?

6. The two ways to live

A. Our way:

- Reject the ruler—God
- Try to run life our own way

Result:

- Condemned by God
- Facing death and judgement

B. God's new way:

- Submit to Jesus as our ruler
- Rely on Jesus' death and resurrection

Result:

- Forgiven by God
- Given eternal life

Whoever believes in the Son has eternal life, but whoever rejects the Son will not see life, for God's wrath remains on him. (John chapter 3, verse 36)

Which of these represents the way you want to live?

Feedback on this resource

We really appreciate getting feedback about our resources—not just suggestions for how to improve them, but also positive feedback and ways they can be used. We especially love to hear that the resources may have helped someone in their Christian growth.

You can send feedback to us via the 'Feedback' menu in our online store, or write to us at info@matthiasmedia.com.au.

Matthias Media is an evangelical publishing ministry that seeks to persuade all Christians of the truth of God's purposes in Jesus Christ as revealed in the Bible, and equip them with high-quality resources, so that by the work of the Holy Spirit they will:

- abandon their lives to the honour and service of Christ in daily holiness and decision-making
- pray constantly in Christ's name for the fruitfulness and growth of his gospel
- speak the Bible's life-changing word whenever and however they can—in the home, in the world and in the fellowship of his people.

Our resources range from Bible studies and books through to training courses, audio sermons and children's Sunday School material. To find out more, and to access samples and free downloads, visit our website:

www.matthiasmedia.com

How to buy our resources

1. Direct from us over the internet:
   – in the US: www.matthiasmedia.com
   – in Australia: www.matthiasmedia.com.au

2. Direct from us by phone: please visit our website for current phone contact information.

3. Through a range of outlets in various parts of the world. Visit **www.matthiasmedia.com/contact** for details about recommended retailers in your part of the world.

4. Trade enquiries can be addressed to:
   – in the US and Canada: sales@matthiasmedia.com
   – in Australia and the rest of the world: sales@matthiasmedia.com.au

Register at our website for our **free** regular email update to receive information about the latest new resources, **exclusive special offers**, and free articles to help you grow in your Christian life and ministry.